CLAIMANTS TO ROYALTY.

CLAIMANTS TO ROYALTY.

BY

JOHN H. INGRAM.

"*Le public qui veut être dupé à tout prix, en était fort satisfait.*"
BOREL.

LONDON:
DAVID BOGUE, 3, ST. MARTIN'S PLACE,
TRAFALGAR SQUARE, W.C.
1882.

Notice

In many older books, foxing (or discoloration) occurs and, in some instances, print lightens with wear and age. Reprinted books, such as this, often duplicate these flaws, notwithstanding efforts to reduce or eliminate them. The pages of this reprint have been digitally enhanced and, where possible, the flaws eliminated in order to provide clarity of content and a pleasant reading experience.

Originally published
London:
1882

Reprinted by:

Janaway Publishing, Inc.
732 Kelsey Ct.
Santa Maria, California 93454
(805) 925-1038
www.janawaygenealogy.com

2014

ISBN: 978-1-59641-320-7

Made in the United States of America

CONTENTS.

	PAGE
INTRODUCTION	vii
THE FALSE SMERDIS OF PERSIA	1
THE FALSE ANTIOCHUS OF SYRIA	10
THE FALSE ALEXANDER BALAS OF SYRIA	12
THE FALSE PHILIP OF MACEDON	17
THE FALSE ALEXANDER OF JERUSALEM	20
THE FALSE NERO OF ROME	25
THE FALSE CLOTAIRE THE SECOND OF FRANCE	29
THE FALSE CLOVIS THE THIRD OF FRANCE	35
THE FALSE SUATOCOPIUS OF MORAVIA	40
THE FALSE HENRY THE FIFTH OF GERMANY	45
THE FALSE ALEXIS, EMPEROR OF THE EAST	47
THE FALSE BALDWIN OF FLANDERS	53
THE FALSE FREDERICK THE SECOND OF GERMANY	61
THE FALSE VOLDEMAR THE SECOND OF BRANDENBURG	68
THE FALSE RICHARD THE SECOND OF ENGLAND	75
THE FALSE MUSTAPHA OF TURKEY	77
THE FALSE EDWARD THE SIXTH OF ENGLAND	86
THE FALSE RICHARD THE FOURTH OF ENGLAND	94
THE FALSE MUSTAPHA THE SECOND OF TURKEY	108

CONTENTS.

	PAGE
THE FALSE SEBASTIAN OF PORTUGAL	113
THE FALSE DEMETRIUS OF RUSSIA	126
THE FALSE DEMETRIUS THE YOUNGER OF RUSSIA	134
THE FALSE ZAGA CHRIST OF ABYSSINIA	144
THE FALSE IBRAHIM OF TURKEY	152
THE FALSE MAHOMET BEY OF TURKEY	158
THE FALSE HERCULES D'ESTE OF MODENA	164
THE FALSE CHARLOTTE OF RUSSIA	174
THE FALSE PETER THE THIRD OF RUSSIA	179
THE FALSE HEREDITARY PRINCE OF BADEN	185
THE FALSE DAUPHINS:—	
HERVAGAULT	203
BRUNEAU	206
HEBERT	211
NAUNDORFF	227
MEVES	230
WILLIAMS	236
THE FALSE PRINCESS OF CUMBERLAND	244
THE FALSE COUNTS OF ALBANY	252

INTRODUCTION.

THE History of Popular Delusions might well have contained another chapter, and that one not calculated to have been the least interesting, devoted to a record of aspirants to the names and titles of deceased persons. The list of claimants to the thrones of defunct monarchs is a lengthy one, the chronicles of nearly every civilized country affording more or less numerous instances of the appearance of these pretenders to royalty. Human credulity has afforded a tempting bait for such impostors: *le public*, as Petrus Borel says, *qui veut être dupé à tous prix, en était fort satisfait*, for the discontented and ambitious have always been numerous enough and willing enough to accept, either as a leader or as a tool, any one sufficiently daring to assert his identity with that of the dead prince.

The subject of this volume should, indeed, possess sufficient attraction in itself, without needing the adventitious aid of any recent *causes célèbres* to give it additional interest. The mystery which envelopes the histories of such men as the supposititious Voldemar of Brandenburg, Perkin Warbeck, the *soi-disant* Sebastian of Portugal, and other renowned claimants to royalty, invests their romantic adventures with a glamour surpassing that of acknowledged fiction. Whether impostors, or the persons they alleged themselves to be, the record of their lives and fate forms one of the most fascinating chapters of historic biography. In many instances the materials procurable are too scanty to admit of lengthy memoirs, whilst even in cases where that is not so, only the most remarkable features of a claimant's story have been selected, in order to render this work as inclusive as possible. In instances of suspicious evidence (and, it must be premised, many of the incidents herein recorded are based upon dubious testimony), only a bare recapitulation of an authority's account is given, all expression of personal opinion being suppressed, and the reader left to form his own theory as to the truth or falsity of the aspirant's claim.

The numerous cases of claimants to royalty herein recorded constitute, it is true, but a portion of those to be met with in history, yet it is believed they include the most interesting. In several instances the evidence preserved of these adventurers' careers is too scanty for separate mention, nevertheless passing allusion may be made to the pseudo Perseus of Macedon, to the false Ariarathes of Cappadocia, and to the remarkable case of Agrippa's slave, who concealed his master's death and assumed his master's position, until the inevitable detection and execution overtook him. In the first and second centuries of the Christian era many of these pretenders sprang up in different portions of the Latin empire, and gave the Romans a great amount of trouble. One of the most noteworthy, considering the long continuance of his success, was a man claiming to be Achelaus, son of Mithridates, King of Pontus. According to the account given by Latin writers, so skilfully did he play his part that the King of Egypt, one of the Ptolemys, actually gave him his daughter in marriage, and appointed him heir and successor to the kingdom of Egypt. This claimant, however, like so many of his class, met with an untimely end, being finally defeated and slain on the battlefield by the Romans, under the Consul Gabrinus.

In the middle ages some curious but not very clearly chronicled instances of these troublesome personages appear. A mysterious case occurred in Sicily in the twelfth century. Roger the Third, dying in 1149, was succeeded by his brother, William the Fourth; and when he expired, in 1186, a man came forward and claimed the crown, under the pretext that he was son of the former monarch. Eventually he was overthrown, and the throne left to the possession of Tancred, the legitimate heir.

In 1570 there was an insurrection against the existing imperial rule in Russia that nearly met with success, and in which one of these pretenders to royalty played an important part. The rebels were led by Stenko, a Cossack chief, and at one time gained such advantages that the entire overthrow of the Romanoff dynasty appeared probable. Alexis, the reigning Czar, had recently lost his eldest son, the heir-apparent, towards whom his feelings were believed to have been anything but paternal. Availing himself of these circumstances, Stenko proclaimed that the Czarewitch was not dead, but had fled to his camp in order to seek refuge from his father's cruelty. A young Circassian, so it is alleged, was employed to personate the prince, whilst another representative was found to personify Nikon, the late patriarch of the Russian Church, who had been deposed and imprisoned by the Czar. The imposture was immensely successful for a time, as multitudes of the High Church party joined the rebels, whose numbers ultimately exceeded one hundred thousand men. Their triumph, however, was but transient, as they were entirely routed by the Imperial troops, whose taste for blood was gratified by the massacre of several thousands of the rebels, among whom, it is presumed, was the personator of the deceased Czarewitch.

The nearer we approach our own time the fewer, it might be anticipated, would be these claimants; but that they have not become an extinct class our pages will show. Not only has there been a nume-

INTRODUCTION. xi

rous and apparently inexhaustible supply of candidates for the name and title of the so-called "Louis the Seventeenth" of France, the little Dauphin who is believed to have perished in the first French revolution, but even quite recently instances have occurred in England of persons claiming to be the hereditary representatives of the royal houses of Stuart and Brunswick. A perusal of the following sketches will prove, however, that only those pretenders have obtained any strong hold upon national feeling who have appeared in times of general dissatisfaction or public calamity, and when the people have been only too willing to swear allegiance to any one having the slightest shadow of authority, and who, at the same time, appeared disposed to rectify their grievances. This will account, to some extent, for a curious phenomenon connected with these claimants, and that is the fact that at certain epochs in history they appear in clusters. In Henry the Seventh's reign it was thus in England; Portugal beheld four Sebastians appear successively; whilst Russia has been quite a hotbed for these mushroom monarchs, having produced, among others, four false Demetriuses and six pseudo Peters.

But enough has been said to prove the richness of the ground now broken, and in leaving this book in the reader's hands, it may be remarked that it is the result of several years' research amid "quaint and curious volumes of forgotten lore;" amid, in some instances, old tomes of considerable rarity. A small portion of this work it should, moreover, be added, was published in the pages of a magazine about ten years ago, but that portion has been thoroughly revised for the present publication.

JOHN H. INGRAM.

CLAIMANTS TO ROYALTY.

THE FALSE SMERDIS OF PERSIA.

B.C. 520.

THE history of no country is more replete with strange incidents and tragic events than is the history of Persia, and probably none of those romantic episodes are more curious than is that of the pseudo Smerdis.

Herodotus is our chief authority for the few circumstances recounted of this impostor's life and deeds, and those few circumstances, like so many other wonderful things told of by the "Father of History," must be taken *cum granô salis*. It is very difficult to distinguish the facts of so remote a period of the world's history as was the epoch of Smerdis from the fable, and the safer plan is to accept all such records, not strongly corroborated by a conformity of contemporary opinion, as pure fiction, or as merely symbolic. The migrations and conquests of prehistoric peoples, as displayed by their philological and ethnological remains, are far more reliable evidence than are fables of the partial, or purposely misleading so-called "historians" of antiquity, whose writings generally are little better than collections of allegorical folk-lore.

The story of the pseudo Smerdis, with these qualifying reservations, may be narrated thus:—Cyrus, the founder of the Persian empire, left his extensive possessions to his eldest son, Cambyses. This monarch, whom it has been sought to identify with the Ahasuerus of Scripture, commenced his reign with a great display of energy and warlike spirit, but would appear to have incensed the priesthoods of the different countries under his sway by manifesting an utter contempt for their rites, and by deriding their ceremonies.

Urged by an insatiable ambition, he made war upon Egypt, added it to his already overgrown empire, and then, with his vast hordes of soldiery, overran the greater portion of North Africa. Not, however, possessing the ability or means of swaying such extended domains, he found himself, after his armies had suffered most frightful loss of life, compelled to retreat from Ethiopia and to return to Egypt. Arriving in this latter country about the period of the festivals held in honour of Apis, he is stated to have slain the sacred bull, under which form the god was symbolically worshipped, and in consequence of the sacrilegious deed, was punished with insanity. Previous to this catastrophe, in a fit of jealousy, he had sent his only brother Smerdis back to Persia; and now his suspicions as to the good faith of his nearest relative and heir were intensified by a dream he had, in which he imagined that a courier had arrived from Persia to inform him that Smerdis had usurped the Persian throne.

Filled with dread, Cambyses sent for Prexaspes, his most faithful servitor, and persuaded him to undertake the assassination of Smerdis. During the absence of his envoy, and whilst under the influence of frightful attacks of mental aberration, he committed the most terrible cruelties, amongst the crimes enumerated by the historian being the brutal murder of his sister, whom he had espoused; the slaying of the son of his favourite, Prexaspes, and the burying alive—head downwards—of twelve of the principal noblemen of his court.

The assassination of Smerdis, which was undoubtedly carried out, combined with the mental incapacity of Cambyses, offered a good opportunity for a bold, energetic man to grasp the reins of power, and, as is generally the case, the man presented himself. There was a certain member of the Magi, or priestly caste of Persia, who not only greatly resembled the murdered prince in feature, but also, more wonderful to relate, bore the same name of Smerdis. *The ears of this man had been cut off* by Cyrus for some crime or offence. He was, therefore, as may be well imagined, only too ready to seize an opportunity to avenge himself on his royal master. Aided, if not instigated, by his elder brother, Patizithes, a man of some influence, and Governor of the Palace, Smerdis raised the standard of revolt, and, the death of the real prince not being generally known, speedily obtained possession of all the royal strongholds. Tutored by his brother, the pseudo prince usurped the throne, and then, as the veritable son of Cyrus, sent envoys to all parts, but chiefly to the chief men and commanders of the army in Egypt, ordering them to relinquish their allegiance to Cambyses, and to do homage to him, Smerdis, as King of Persia.

One of the pretender's envoys having arrived at Ecbatana, in Syria, where the Persian monarch was, proclaimed his mission publicly in the midst of the army. When Cambyses heard the announcement he fancied that he had been deceived by Prexaspes, and that he had not executed his order to kill Smerdis. He angrily accused his too faithful servitor of having betrayed him, but he not only positively assured him that he had done the deed, and buried the murdered prince with his own hands, but also suggested to him that the envoy should be sent after and interrogated. This reasonable advice being approved of by Cambyses, the messenger was at once sought for, discovered, brought before the king, and promised a safe conduct if he confessed the truth.

"Have you seen Prince Smerdis personally?" demanded Prexaspes. "Have you received your instructions from his own mouth, or from one of his ministers?"

"Verily," answered the man, "I have not beheld Prince Smerdis since the Egyptian war; but the Magi, who was made governor of the palace by Cambyses, gave me my orders, and informed me that Smerdis, the son of Cyrus, had commanded that the proclamation should be published here."

Cambyses, on hearing this, exonerated his confidant from the charge of having disobeyed his orders, but could not comprehend the meaning of the conspiracy against his authority. Prexaspes, however, who was well acquainted with the Magi brothers, began to see through the mystery, and said:

"This affair is brought about by the Magi, who are always conspiring against you. Patizithes, whom you left in Persia to take charge of your affairs and his brother Smerdis, are the authors of this undertaking."

Cambyses, on hearing the name of Smerdis pronounced, called to mind his dream, and perceiving the inutility of his fratricidal crime, began to bewail his brother's death. Determined to set forth at once to expose and punish the pretender, he hastily mounted his horse, and in so doing the scabbard becoming detached from the sword, the naked weapon penetrated his right thigh, exactly in the same way as he had mortally wounded the sacred bull of Apis!

Finding himself severely wounded, the king demanded the name of the place, and being informed that it was Ecbatana, at once concluded that his end was near at hand, an oracle having formerly foretold that he would die at Ecbatana. He had hitherto believed that the prophecy meant the town of that name in Media, but now saw that it meant Ecbatana in Syria.

After lingering in a serious state for some days, he summoned the chief Persian nobles who were with him, and said: "I must confess to you what, above all things, I would have kept concealed. When in Egypt I had a dream which made me fear that my brother Smerdis would despoil me of the empire; I therefore had him executed. But his death has but hastened the loss of my sovereignty, for it was the Magi Smerdis of whom God spoke to me in a dream, and who has now taken up arms against me. Do not imagine that it is Smerdis, the son of Cyrus, still living; but, believe me, the kingdom has been usurped by the Magi, one of whom I left in Persia to manage my household affairs, and the other is his brother named Smerdis." He then conjured them to take vengeance upon the pretenders, and with some shrewd injunctions, took leave of them. After this interview his wound rapidly became mortal, and he died after a reign of little more than seven years.

Upon the decease of Cambyses, no one cared to dispute possession of the Persian throne with the pseudo Smerdis, who was, indeed, generally believed to be the prince whose name he had assumed, most people deeming the dying words of the late monarch to have been prompted by a desire for vengeance upon his brother for seeking the Persian sovereignty during his life. As for Prexaspes, for obvious reasons he refrained from proclaiming his share in the death of a son of Cyrus.

For seven months the pretender ruled this mighty empire, and with such beneficence and justice that for long after his death he was deeply regretted by all the peoples of Asia, with the exception of the warlike Persians, whom he offended by exempting all his subjects from military service for three years, and from all kinds of tribute. In the eighth month of his reign his imposture was thus singularly discovered. Otanes, a Persian nobleman of the highest rank and wealth, had long suspected the deceit, and by means of his daughter Phædyma was enabled to detect it. She had been wife to the late king, and after the death of Cambyses was retained in the impostor's harem. Otanes knew that the Magian Smerdis, whom he guessed the impersonator of the dead prince to be, had had his ears cut off. He therefore commanded his daughter to try and discover, during his slumbers, whether the present wearer of the crown had lost his or not. The girl consented, and, despite all the pretender's care to conceal his deficiency, in the course of a few days was enabled to inform her father that this Smerdis *had not any ears.* This intelligence was sufficient for Otanes, who summoned six of the leading Persian nobles, and informed them of his discovery. Whilst they were debating amongst themselves how to take vengeance upon the Magians, another unlooked-for event hastened the pretender's detection.

Feeling insecure, the party of the pseudo Smerdis summoned to them Prexaspes, the only man who could prove the death of the murdered prince, and by means of heavy bribes sought to win him to their party. Knowing his influence amongst the people, and his knowledge of the private affairs of the late king, they desired him to acknowledge the present occupant of the throne as the veritable son and heir of Cyrus. He appeared to consent. The Persians were required to assemble, and Prexaspes, addressing them from the summit of an adjacent tower, frustrated all the Magi's plans by confessing himself to the multitude as the assassin of the real Smerdis, the son of Cyrus the King. As soon as he had completed the story of the murder, he implored them to oust the Magians from power, and then precipitating himself from the tower, was killed on the spot.

In the meanwhile the seven Persian noblemen were not idle. Having arranged their plans, they penetrated into the palace, slew the body-guards, and, despite their courageous resistance, put the pretender and his brother to death. Thus, after a most prosperous reign of eight months, perished the pseudo Smerdis. His death was followed by a general attack upon the Magi, or so-called "wise men;" and a very large number of them were ruthlessly slaughtered. The fact of their being Medes rendered them hateful to the Persians, and caused the latter to be only too glad of an excuse for their extermination.

THE FALSE ANTIOCHUS OF SYRIA.

B.C. 186.

A PRETENDER to the name and titles of Antiochus, surnamed the Great, King of Syria, is mentioned by several ancient historians as having appeared after the death of that monarch. There is an unfathomable mystery, however, about the whole affair. This celebrated sovereign having acquired considerable renown by his wars against the Romans, and his efforts on behalf of Greek freedom, eventually falsified his subjects' expectation by giving way to all kinds of debaucheries and enervating excesses. The last scene of his life's tragedy, which followed fast upon his misdoings, is so variously stated by different writers, that it is absolutely impossible to extract the truth from their divers accounts. He is generally supposed, after having been defeated and put to flight by the Romans, to have been assassinated. Pliny the Younger asserts that after his overthrow he fled to Mount Tamus, and there endeavoured to drown his troubles in wine; but that at last, growing quarrelsome and tyrannical towards the companions of his debaucheries, they one day put an end to his existence. Whatever may have been the manner of this monarch's death, all historians agree that after that event an impostor named Artemion was induced by the wife of the deceased king to come forward and pretend that he was Antiochus. Solinus states that this man was of ignoble birth, whilst according to other authors, he was a relative of the late monarch. Instructed by the queen, he appealed to the people to protect the interests of his putative wife and children; and the people, believing in his identity, at once declined to elect any one for sovereign not approved of by the queen, and she (Laodice), if Pliny's somewhat ambiguous terms are read rightly, placed the diadem upon the head of Artemion. Nothing is recorded of his subsequent fate.

ALEXANDER BALAS OF SYRIA.

B.C. 149.

IN some respects more fortunate than many of his successors in the art of claiming royal kinship, Alexander Balas has obtained the sanction of several Jewish and Roman historians to the legality of his pretensions. In his "Antiquities of the Jews," Josephus, from obvious nationalistic reasons, accepts without a query the pseudo Alexander as the legitimate sovereign of Syria; and more recent Latin chroniclers have copied his narration without doubting—probably without having heard anything to the contrary. Justin, and other later writers, however, positively assert that the real name of this pretender was Prompale; and that so far from having been born in the purple, his parents were of the very lowest ranks of society.

According to these more reliable authorities, Balas was a Rhodian youth employed by various monarchs hostile to the pretensions of Demetrius Soter, then in possession of the kingdom of Syria, to personate Alexander, a long deceased son of Antiochus Epiphanos. The impostor, assuming the name and title of the deceased prince, speedily found himself, through the assistance of the allied sovereigns and the favour of the Roman senate, at the head of a large army, with which he invaded Syria. The garrison of Ptolemais having been betrayed into his hands, and other advantages accruing to him by reason of the hatred which the Syrians entertained for Demetrius, awoke that king to the real danger of the situation. He sent an embassy with rich gifts, and still richer promises, to Jonathan, the Jewish ruler, in order to obtain his friendly assistance, and then, collecting his forces, marched against Balas.

The pretender was not ignorant of the great value of Jonathan's services, and by means of greater presents and more flattering promises managed to withdraw him from an alliance with Demetrius. With the loans obtained from his allies, and by means of extortion, Balas was enabled to gather a large army of mercenary soldiers together, with which to give battle to the Syrian monarch. After a hardly-contested fight Demetrius was slain, and the kingdom fell an easy prey into the hands of the victor, who, elated with his triumph, demanded the hand of Cleopatra, daughter of Ptolemy Philopater, King of Egypt, declaring that as he had now recovered the principality of his forefathers, he was worthy of his alliance. The Egyptian monarch, pleased with this offer, replied that he would meet Alexander at Ptolemais, and there give him his daughter in marriage.

The meeting soon afterwards took place, and the new king was united in marriage to the Princess Cleopatra, receiving with his bride a right royal dower. Jonathan, the Jew, assisted at the wedding *fêtes*, and was very cordially and magnificently treated by the two monarchs. A short time, however, and the impostor began to show the cloven hoof. He commenced his almost unaccountable perfidies by an attempt to overthrow Jonathan, but his forces being defeated by that skilful warrior, he repudiated the affair as carried out without his sanction, and pretended to be pleased with the want of success of his own troops. Aroused from the voluptuousness and profligacy into which he had plunged by the intelligence of an invasion of his dominions by Demetrius, a son of the late king of that name, he prepared for war. About this time he treacherously endeavoured to destroy his father-in-law, Ptolemy, by means of Ammonius, a friend of his; the plot being discovered, Ptolemy wrote to Alexander, and demanded that condign punishment should be administered to Ammonius, but when he found that his demands were disregarded, he soon perceived whence the conspiracy had originated, and repented of having given his daughter in marriage to the pseudo Alexander. Having succeeded in getting the princess back into his own hands, he broke off his alliance with her husband, and at once entered into a league of mutual assistance and friendship with the young Demetrius, to whom he subsequently offered his daughter in marriage.

This prince was only too delighted with the terms of the embassage, and, without troubling himself as to the existence of Balas's prior claim, gladly accepted the hand of Cleopatra, coupled as it was with the armed assistance of her father. After some difficulty the Egyptian king persuaded the people of Antioch to receive Demetrius as their king, and then took the field with a force capable of supporting his new son-in-law's claims.

In the meanwhile Balas was not idle; but, hastening into Syria from Cecilia, where he was when the war broke out, he collected a large army, and, in right royal fashion, burnt and pillaged the country belonging to Antioch. Forced to give battle to the combined strength of Ptolemy and his son-in-law (for Demetrius had already espoused his antagonist's wife), the pretender was, however, beaten and put to flight. Seeking refuge in Arabia, his head was cut off by Zabdiel, an Arabian prince, and sent to Ptolemy. The Egyptian monarch, however, did not long enjoy his triumph, for shortly after the arrival of the head of his first son-in-law, he died from the effect of the wounds received in defeating him. For five years the pseudo Alexander reigned over a large portion of Asia, during which period he thoroughly disgusted his subjects by his absurd vanity and profligate conduct.

Some years after the death of Balas, Diodotus Tryphon, one of his commanders, finding the nation as dissatisfied with Demetrius as they had been with Alexander, excited a rebellion against him, and set up a son, or a pretended son, of his late master as king. Tryphon ultimately proving victorious over Demetrius, and obtaining the entire control of the country, put his youthful *protégé* to death, and, according to the account of Livy and Josephus, usurped the government himself; but after a reign of three years was overthrown and slain.

THE FALSE PHILIP OF MACEDON.

B.C. 144.

THE condition of Greece after the usurpation of supreme power by Philip of Macedon and his son, Alexander the Great, was truly deplorable, and, despite the despairing efforts of the Achaian League to resuscitate the expiring liberties of the glorious old republics, grew rapidly from bad to worse. Finally, the spirit of its people broken, their freedom destroyed, and national feeling extinguished, the cradle of European civilization fell an easy prey to the omnivorous greed of Rome.

A later Philip of Macedon incurred the anger of the Romans by forming a league with Hannibal, the Carthaginian, and after suffering terrible reverses in the wars which ensued, was compelled to accept peace upon the most humiliating terms, including the surrender of several entire provinces; of his navy, and the payment of a heavy indemnity to the conquerors. Twelve years after the death of this monarch (B.C. 178), his son and successor, Perseus, recommenced hostilities with the Romans. After a long series of alternate victories and defeats, this last and most unfortunate of the Macedonian kings was overthrown at the battle of Pydna by Æmilius, the Roman consul, and sent captive, with his children, to Rome.

About twenty years later, or B.C. 149, and whilst the Macedonians were still newly smarting under the yoke of the victors, a man presented himself to the people as Philip, their late king. Livy, whose account we must chiefly follow, states that this impostor was generally reputed to have been a slave; in history he is known as Andriscus the Pretender. Our chief authority acknowledges that he manifested a truly royal courage, and that he was found to greatly resemble the monarch whose name and dignity he claimed, but who had died nearly thirty years previously. Incautiously underrating the power of this Andriscus, who was well supported by the despairing Macedonians, the Romans contented themselves with sending a few troops, under the Pretor Juventius, against the insurgents, and consequently sustained a severe defeat, in which an entire legion and the Pretor himself were completely cut to pieces. This success was short-lived. The Consul Metellus taking the field overthrew and pursued Andriscus to the Thracian mountains, and compelled a neighbouring prince, with whom he had taken refuge, to deliver him into his hands. The capture of this impostor was made an occasion for a great triumph by the Romans, who rejoiced as much—records the historian—as if they had acquired possession of the person of a veritable king. His future story is not known, but the unfortunate country which had placed itself under his guidance was, as is but too well known, completely subjugated, and its people reduced to a state of servitude, from the effects of which they never recovered. It is worthy of note that after the overthrow of Andriscus, two or three pseudo Philips from time to time came forward to agitate the country, trouble the Roman rulers, and still further degrade the people; but none of them ever displayed the same courageous bearing, or attained to such notoriety as he did.

THE FALSE ALEXANDER OF JERUSALEM.

A.D 3.

IN the foremost ranks of classic claimants may be placed the false Alexander, who claimed the Jewish crown under the pretence of being a son of Herod Antipas. Herod, although tributary to the Roman empire, raised the Jewish kingdom to a higher pitch of grandeur than it had reached since the days of Solomon. Great, however, as were his military successes, and extraordinary the pomp and magnificence of his court, his tyranny and cruelty render the annals of his lengthy reign almost unreadable. The record of his crimes, as detailed by Josephus, equals in enormity the worst page of Roman history.

Amongst the relatives whom he singled out to inflict death upon were three of his own sons. Having accused his two sons by his second wife, the beautiful Marianne, of having plotted against his crown, he had them both arrested and condemned to death. After the barbarous execution of an old soldier, Tero, who had nobly pleaded the cause of the imprisoned princes, he sent them both—Alexander and Aristobulus—to Sebaste, a city in the vicinity of Cæsarea, and caused them to be there strangled. After the execution of his sons, whose lives Herod had so embittered that, guilty or not of the terrible accusation made against them, their fate was deplored by many of their countrymen, he had their dead bodies brought to Alexandrium, and buried by the side of their maternal grandfather, Alexander.

About twelve years after the tragic death of the princely brothers, and when Herod himself had died in the horrible manner described by Josephus, the Hebrew nation, subdivided by its Roman lord, and infested by hordes of robbers, afforded a good opening for a royal claimant; and accordingly one appeared.

A Jew resident in Sidon, greatly resembling Alexander, the elder of the deceased brothers, in features, was persuaded by a Roman freedman, with whom he had been brought up, to personate the late prince. Before airing his pretensions, the claimant obtained the assistance of a countryman of his who was well versed in the affairs of the kingdom, and under his instructions the pseudo Alexander came forth from his obscurity with a plausible story of how the persons commissioned to execute him and his brother Aristobulus had compassion upon them, and putting dead bodies in their place, had allowed them to escape. As usual, a credulous multitude believed in the impostor, and from the Cretan Jews he and his fellow plotters reaped a rich harvest. Furnished with money, he next sailed to Mitylene, where he obtained a further supply of cash, and persuaded some of the believers in his identity to accompany him to Rome, where he probably expected the Emperor Augustus would assist him to obtain possession of the kingdom of Judea; although Josephus strangely asserts that he went to Rome in hopes of avoiding detection.

On landing at Pozzuoli, near Naples, he was received by the Jews resident there in truly regal manner, and treated in every respect as if he were really the legitimate son and successor of Herod. Many persons who had been personally acquainted with Prince Alexander positively asserted his identity with the claimant. Accompanied by a large concourse of people, and bearing with him his accumulated costly gifts, the impostor entered Rome in regal state, the whole of the Jews in the city going out in a body to welcome him.

Augustus Cæsar would appear to have suspected the deceit from the first, but allowing the common belief to have some weight with him, he sent Celadus, to whom Alexander had been well known, to bring the pseudo prince to him. " Directly the emperor saw the claimant," says Josephus, "he discerned a difference in his countenance; and when he had discovered that his whole body was of a more robust texture and like that of a slave, he understood the whole was a contrivance." The emperor, however, in order to thoroughly sift the strange matter, cross-questioned the pseudo prince, asking him what had become of his brother Aristobulus, who, he had stated, was saved also, and why they did not appear together. The impudent impostor replied that his brother had been left in the Isle of Cyprus, for fear of treachery, as, if separated, it would be more difficult for their enemies to make away with both of them.

Augustus, getting weary of the conspiracy, took the claimant aside, and said to him privately: " Do not think to abuse my credulity as you have done with so many. I am not deceived. Frankly confess the whole truth, and I give you my word to spare your life. Tell me who you are, and what prompted you to engage in this plot, for this is too considerable a piece of villany for one of your age to have undertaken alone."

Seeing that there was no chance of escape, the pretender discovered the whole affair to the emperor, pointing out to him the Jew who, noticing his likeness to the murdered prince, had persuaded him to engage in the daring undertaking; whose object in the contrivance of the plot, says our principal authority, being only to get money, in which respect he had so far succeeded that "he had received more presents in every city than ever Alexander did when he was alive."

Augustus could not forbear laughing at the man's story; but, for all his merriment, did not restrain his anger. He had promised the pretender his life, and, therefore, spared it; but he put him amongst his rowers, doubtless deeming him fitter to wield an oar than a sceptre. The contriver of the plot, however, had to expiate his cleverness with his life, and was crucified,—a usual method, in those days, of executing important criminals.

THE FALSE NERO OF ROME.

A.D. 73.

ABOUT two years after the death of Nero, the Roman empire was startled by the report that a man claiming to be the deceased monarch, and closely resembling him in form and features, had appeared in the East, with the proclaimed intention of resuming the crown which had been wrested from him by an unjust and felonious act of the Senate. Tacitus, who has left the most circumstantial account of this impostor's story, declares him to have been a slave of Pontus in Asia; but, according to others, he was originally an Italian freeman. Many different rumours spread through the various provinces of the empire, causing great alarm, especially in Greece and Asia, where the Roman power was not yet thoroughly consolidated, many persons firmly believing, and many feigning to believe, that Nero was still living. John Zonaras, in the second book of his Greek annals, confirms the account given by Tacitus, and avers the pretender's name to have been Terentius Maximus.

This pseudo Cæsar, having deceived many people by his resemblance to the deceased emperor, speedily collected a multitude of rogues, vagabonds, and fugitives, and having engaged them in his service by means of grand promises, put to sea. Driven by a tempest on to the shore of the Island of Delos, he succeeded in gaining over some soldiery there, who were returning from the East, and with this reinforcement was enabled to despoil the various traders sheltering in the port of their merchandize, and to arm all the most resolute of the slaves. He endeavoured, by all means at his command, to acquire the confidence of Siana, a centurion of the Syrian army, who was deputed by the Syrians to go to Rome, to make a treaty with the Pretorian cohorts, or regiments of the guards. He urged this captain so much that he was compelled to quit the island and fly, in order to escape the danger with which he was threatened. This proceeding of the officer greatly increased the fear which the name of the pseudo Nero began to inspire, and caused many other discontented spirits to take service under him. There is no knowing to what extent his power might have increased, had not chance found an opportunity of causing his overthrow.

The late Emperor Galba had bestowed the government of Galatia and Pamphilia upon Calphurnius

Asprenas; two galleys from the fleet, which was at Misena, had received orders to escort him to his new post. They anchored off the coast of Delos, without, however, disembarking their crews. Perceiving this, the pretender had a great desire to obtain possession of these two galleys, but not being able to effect his purpose by force, he had recourse to a ruse. He embarked on board a vessel, in order to reconnoitre the strange sails himself, and to learn who they were, never dreaming that there was the governor of a province on board. He appeared at the prow of his vessel, and in his assumed character movingly conjured the soldiers who appeared in the galleys to be faithful to their oath of fidelity, which they had formerly sworn to him their Emperor, Nero.

The pilots refused to have anything to do with him, saying they were not the masters; but whilst they thus kept him engaged in conversation, they informed Calphurnius of what was passing, and on representing to him the small dimensions of the vessel in which the aspirant to imperialism appeared, he gave instructions for it to be attacked. The false Nero, caught in his own snare, fought like a lion, but at last, being overcome, he killed himself.

His corse, remarkable for its large eyes and

beautiful hair, and, above all, for its ferocity of visage, was carried through Asia to Rome, where every one was allowed to see it, and admire the daring of him who had attempted to usurp, by means of a bold imposture, the most powerful empire of the universe.

THE FALSE CLOTAIRE THE SECOND OF FRANCE.

A.D. 583.

THE story of this claimant's adventures is, perhaps, the most romantic of all our heroes, but unfortunately it is one of the most unreliable. The Mezerays and other ancient writers, however, give the tale as authentic, and as they recount it so it is detailed here; fact and fiction being difficult in such cases to disentangle.

This pretender is styled in history Gondebaud, and would appear to have had some real claims to a royal origin, his mother having educated him from his earliest infancy as the king's son, and carefully preserved from the desecrating shears his flowing locks—a mark of regal birth amongst the ancient Franks.

Clotaire the First, who was then reigning at Soissons, refused to accept the imputed parentage, and the woman accordingly fled with the child to Paris, to claim the protection of Childebert, the king's brother, who was reigning there. Childebert, not having any male children of his own, took a liking to the boy, and was desirous of adopting him as his nephew, and educating him at his court; but when the putative father heard this he was greatly incensed, and wrote to his brother to send Gondebaud to him, as he would take care of him, adding that it was false to call him his son, which he was not; that educating him as a king's son was giving the boy honours to which he was not entitled, and might hereafter afford him an opportunity of deceiving the world. Clotaire's care was the more necessary as illegitimacy did not, amongst the ancient Franks, debar the offspring's right to the crown.

The king of Soissons having obtained possession of his supposed son, had his head shaved and sent him into a monastery. Dying, however, in 561, his eldest son, Cherebert, who succeeded him, took compassion upon Gondebaud, and, during the whole of his reign, treated him with fraternal kindness. Cherebert dying in 570, the crown passed to Sigobert, who ordered our hero to come to his court. He at once obeyed, was seized, his flowing locks again severed from his head, and he once more imprisoned in a monastery. Finding means of escape, the unfortunate youth fled into Italy, and made his way to the camp of Narses, the Emperor Justinian's famous general.

By Narses, Gondebaud was kindly received and promised succour; but just at the moment when he seemed on the point of being enabled to take the field against his presumed relatives, his protector died, and he was left once more a friendless wanderer. In the meantime, the Emperor Justinian had also died, and his successors, Justin the Second and Sophia, determined to give the remains of their renowned warrior, Narses, a superb funeral. Our claimant availed himself of the opportunity to make his court to the imperial couple, and travelled with the body to Constantinople, where he was extremely well received, his handsome figure and courtier-like manner obtaining him no little favour from the empress.

Gondebaud dwelt at the Constantinopolitan court during the reigns of Justin the Second and his successor Tiberius. With Maurice, general and subsequently successor of the latter, he served in several campaigns against the Persians, and apparently with credit. He would probably have ended his days honourably in the Eastern Empire had not a certain conspirator, Boson, tempted him to return to France with the information that his supposed brother Sigobert had been treacherously murdered; that the two infamous queens, Brunechild and Fredegonde, had completely disorganized the country with their crimes and quarrels; adding, that the time was ripe for his return, the people being only too desirous of submitting to his rule, and that the two kings who now divided the country between them, being childless, would not offer any great opposition to his claims. Deceived by these specious arguments, Gondebaud, after a sojourn of twenty years in the Orient, returned to France, taking with him good equipments and a large sum of money, advanced by his friend the Emperor Tiberius.

Landing at Marseilles, he was received by the bishop of that city with great honours, and the news of his arrival having spread abroad, coupled with the rumour that he was accompanied by enormous wealth, the result of having discovered the supposed hoard of Narses, caused large numbers of people, including many of high rank, to come to his camp to pay homage. In addition to their expectation of bountiful gifts from his hands, his visitors found Gondebaud good-looking, and apparently worthy of the warlike reputation he had obtained from having served under Narses and Maurice. The Duke of Toulouse and other independent nobles proffered their alliance; so that after all his tussles with fortune our hero seemed at last nearly certain of a kingdom. But at this critical moment the traitor Boson turned against him, and, seizing his treasures, compelled

Gondebaud to fly, and take refuge in an impregnable island at the mouth of the Rhone.

After having thus endured the ups and downs of fickle fortune, this claimant, in hopes of ingratiating himself with the Franks, and at the suggestion of his ally Childebert, king of Metz, took upon himself the pseudo name of Clotaire, thus more distinctly marking his claim to the throne of his putative father Clotaire the First. But all the arts of the pretender were unavailable to obtain the assistance or recognition of Gontran, king of Orleans, who took up arms in defence of the real heir to the throne, the veritable Clotaire the Second, a child of tender years, and who, despite the fact that Gondebaud's forces were commanded by the best generals of the country, by fight or stratagem gradually deprived him of all his treasures, allies, and, finally, of his life. For the pretender's chief adherents finding that Gontran was determined to resist him to the uttermost, and probably seeing little prospect of his ultimately obtaining any permanent power in the country, determined to abandon Gondebaud to his fate; he was, however, so strongly fortified, and so well provided with every necessary of war in his stronghold, that his foes found the only method of dislodging him was by stratagem.

Gontran accordingly got Queen Brunechild, the

mother of his adopted heir, Childebert, to write to our hero, under the pretence of her being secretly in his interest, and advise him to remove with all his treasure to Bordeaux, where he would have the command of both land and sea. Duped by this woman, the unfortunate claimant forsook his refuge, and put himself *en route* for Bordeaux. On the road he fell in with an ambuscade of the enemy's, which succeeded in stripping him of all the treasure he had accumulated, but did not prevent him arriving at his destination.

Bordeaux sustained a siege of some weeks on the pretender's account, but during the whole of that time traitors in and out of the city were bargaining for his betrayal. At last, his chief men, thinking to ransom their lives with his, persuaded the pseudo Clotaire to go outside the city to confer with the foe as to the terms of peace, and as soon as he was without the walls they closed the gates upon him, leaving him to his fate. He was seized by the besiegers and dragged on to a hillock outside their camp, where he was flung down by one of their commanders; and as the unhappy man was still rolling, the traitor Boson beat out his brains with a battle-axe. Thus perished this luckless pretender to the throne of the Franks, whether a son or not of Clotaire the First, equally unfortunate.

THE FALSE CLOVIS THE THIRD OF FRANCE.

A.D. 676.

WHEN Clotaire the Third came to the French throne he was only five years old; consequently the affairs of the kingdom had to be entrusted to the guidance of a regent. The man selected to fill this post was Ebroin, and the choice appeared in every respect admirable. Ebroin was not only, apparently, fitted by birth and talent to sway the people, but he also possessed the qualification most desirable of all others for the time and clime in which he lived; that is to say, he was a valiant and experienced warrior.

Associated, however, with him in power, was Batilde, the queen dowager, a woman, according to all the priestly chroniclers, of great beauty and discretion, but doubtless much swayed by bigoted ecclesiastics. For some years the country enjoyed considerable prosperity: Batilde ruled with prudence and justice, and by keeping on good terms with the prelates has obtained no little historic fame; whilst

Ebroin, having managed to quarrel with the Church, has left a reputation for all that is bad.

The queen dowager, either by compulsion or inclination, having resigned the cares of government, and taken refuge in the convent of Chelles, the chief minister, Ebroin, or *Maire du Palais*, as he was styled, was enabled to give full vent to all those evil qualities which circumstances had hitherto compelled him to conceal. Taking the entire power into his own hands, he killed and ill-treated, confiscated and exiled, with as much arrogance as a reigning king. In the year 668 the boy Clotaire died, aged about eighteen; and Ebroin, contrary to the wish of the nobles, placed Thierry, the younger brother of the deceased monarch, upon the throne, to the exclusion of the elder brother, Childerick, the next heir. He was induced to act thus in consequence of Thierry's youth, he being but eight, affording him a good opportunity of retaining the governing power in his own hands. In this act, however, he erred; for the nation, or at all events a powerful portion of it, revolted against his authority, overthrew him, and took both him and the prince Thierry prisoners. More merciful than was the wont in those days, the victors put neither of their prisoners to death, but contented themselves with shaving Ebroin's head—then deemed a terrible degradation—and confining him in a monastery, and with placing his youthful *protégé* under priestly surveillance.

In 973, Childerick the Second, and his wife and child, were assassinated by a gentleman whom he had had brutally beaten for remonstrating with him somewhat freely on the danger of an excessive imposition that he had wished to establish. Taking advantage of the confusion into which the country was thrown by this sudden event, Ebroin made his escape from the monastery in which he had been immured, and, aided by a large number of malcontents, set up the standard of revolt against Thierry the Third, who now, in consequence of his brother's death, became the legitimate king. Ebroin was joined by the Governor of Austrasia, by two deposed bishops, and by many other influential men, all of whom shared with him an intense hatred of Leger, Bishop of Autun, who now held the reins of power. In order to obtain more partisans amongst the people, Ebroin and his comrades brought forward a lad of about twelve or thirteen years of age, and asserted that he was a son of Clotaire the Third, who was believed to have died in 670, in his nineteenth year.

There was just a possibility of this boy having been Clotaire's son, although an illegitimate one, no proof of the deceased monarch's marriage ever having been adduced; and as illegitimacy was not in those days deemed a bar to the crown, the claim of little Clovis the Third, as Ebroin had him styled, may have been as valid as that of his competitors. Be that as it may, historians have also termed this youthful pretender, or rather tool of the conspirators, the *false* Clovis. The lad was attired in royal robes, and taught to affect a majesty of deportment towards all those who came to render him homage, whilst all those who refused to acknowledge him as king were maltreated, and their goods seized by his followers. His reign, however, was of short duration. Bishop Leger having been captured, deprived of sight, and thrown into prison, the great nobles and chieftains succumbed at once, and Ebroin found the whole power of the country in his own hands; he, therefore, deemed it better to make terms with Thierry, who willingly replaced him in his post of *Maire du Palais*, conditionally upon being left in nominal possession of the sovereignty.

Having thus attained his purpose, Ebroin had no longer any need of his puppet, and at once relinquished the imposture; but what afterwards became of the boy king history does not relate. As regards the originator of the scheme, his cruelties and tyranny increased daily, so that when in 683, or three or four years after the re-establishment of his power, he was assassinated by a noble named Bermenfroy, whose property he had seized, and whose life he had menaced, it must have been a real relief to his country. Through Ebroin's death it was that a way was opened for the family of Pepin, the founder of the Carlovingian race, to acquire the dignity of *Maire du Palais*, and subsequently the monarchy of France.

SUATOCOPIUS OF MORAVIA.

A.D. 800.

To many casual readers it may seem a singular circumstance that nearly every claimant to regal paternity has found authors, more or less numerous, to espouse his cause, and assert his identity with the monarch whose name he laid claim to. On inspection the singularity vanishes. Putting on one side the difficulties of investigation which ancient annalists had to encounter, and as a rule the defective evidence they had to judge by, the undeniable fact is arrived at that not a few of the so-called historians often wilfully misrepresented, falsified, omitted, and even invented *facts* to suit their own party views.

Many of these forgeries the acumen and research of later ages have exposed; many more will doubtless, in course of time, be discovered, but a still larger number in all probability linger undetected in the pages of history, and will ever remain so. It is unfortunate that the class of men to whom we are compelled to resort chiefly for historic and social information prior to the invention of printing, are the very men whose writings it is necessary to hold in greatest doubt ; and it is, beyond dispute, well ascertained that history which had to filter through a priest's brains, as a rule descended to posterity deeply tinged, to say the best of it, with the hue its author wished it to have in the eyes of the world.

Æneas Sylvius Piccolomini, better known as Pius the Second, amongst his numerous works left a *History of Bohemia*, and the thirteenth chapter of that history details the events which have caused us to insert amongst the claimants to royalty the name of Suatocopius, leaving the reader to decide for himself as to the credibility of the aspirant's claim to the name and title of the supposed slain monarch.

The Marcomanni, or Moravians, are asserted to have been converted to Christianity about the middle of the ninth century by Methodius and Cyril, two Greek monks. These two men, noted in history for having implanted the Christian faith in Russia, Bulgaria, and the adjacent lands, were brothers, members of an illustrious Thessalonican family, and distinguished for their learning and the purity of their lives. About the year 860 these missionaries are stated to have appeared at the court of Suatocopius, a king whose sway was more or less acknowledged, not only by the Moravians, but also, according to priestly authority, by the Hungarians, Bohemians, Poles, and inhabitants of Black Russia, but who, notwithstanding the extent of his territories and the number of his subjects, was tributary to the Emperor of Germany, as had been his predecessors since the days of Charlemagne.

Converted by the Greek brothers to the Christian religion, Suatocopius is stated for many years to have set a good example to his subjects of all the virtues called royal; but finally, emboldened by the continuous prosperity of a long reign and the representations of his courtiers, he declined paying any more tribute into the imperial exchequer. This refusal at once involved him in warfare with the Emperor Arnulph, and in a battle which ensued the Moravians were defeated, and, so it was universally believed, their monarch slain. The body of Suatocopius could not be discovered, declares our chief authority, but the fact of his death was deemed indisputable, and his son was permitted by his godfather, the victor, to ascend the vacant throne.

Many years elapsed, and Suatocopius was probably forgotten, when some monks brought his son the astounding information that his father, the king, had only just expired, in the distant and mean hermitage whence they came. The tale which they told, and which their hearer placed entire credence in, according to the history of Pope Pius, was to the effect that for several years they had housed and fed a wanderer who one day had besought their hospitality; during the whole time he had lived with them he had cheerfully and patiently endured all the hardships of their rough and indigent life, but finding his end approaching, the unknown had summoned them to his side and said:—

"Until the present moment you have not known who I am. Know then that I am the King of Moravia, who, having lost a battle, took refuge amongst you. I die, after having tasted the joys of reigning and of private life. The royal state is certainly not preferable to the repose of solitude. Here I sleep without fear and without disquietude, enjoying the calm and pleasures of life, tasting fruits and the purest water, which is far more agreeable than the most precious beverages the courts of kings afford. I have spent with you happily the remainder of the life God has granted me, and the time which I passed upon the throne now seems to me to have been a continual death. . . . When I am dead inter my body in this place, but go, I beg you, and inform my son, if he be still alive, what I have told you."

Soon after this confession the supposed king died; his body was duly interred by his fellow monks, and information of his decease sent to the reigning monarch. He, with all diligence, had the body disinterred and brought to Volgrade, the capital of

Moravia, and, notwithstanding the years that had elapsed since the disappearance of Suatocopius, and the length of time the corpse had been buried, recognized the body as his father's, and had it deposited, with all due pomp and ceremony, in the royal sepulchre, to moulder, royal or plebeian, amid the ashes of his predecessors.

THE FALSE HENRY THE FIFTH OF GERMANY.

A.D. 1130.

HENRY THE FIFTH of Germany, like so many other monarchs of the middle ages, had wrested the imperial crown from the head of his unfortunate father, Henry the Fourth. This latter emperor, having been dethroned by his unnatural son, took refuge with the Bishop of Liege, in whose city he died of grief.

The fifth Henry was fully recompensed for his undutiful conduct by the continual rebellion of his subjects in different portions of the imperial dominions, by the bitter hostility of his former friend, Archbishop Albert, of Mainz, and by the unceasing persecution of the Papacy. Henry the Fifth died childless in 1125, worn out with strife, and the sceptre passed into the hands of Lothaire the Second. Five years after the Emperor's death, a Benedictine monk of the Abbey of Cluny, in Burgundy, startled his brother recluses by the assertion that he was the supposed deceased monarch, Henry the Fifth of Germany. He declared that being desirous of abdicating the crown which he had forced his unhappy parent to resign to him, he had spread the false intelligence of his own decease, and then had set out, in pilgrim garb, for the Holy Land. He narrated a pitiful tale of the indignities heaped upon his imperial head during the years of his pilgrimage; how he had narrowly escaped drowning through a man having brutally pushed him into the sea when he was on the point of embarkation; how he had been compelled by the Knights Templars, at Acre, to assist as a labourer at the construction of fortifications there; and many other equally edifying stories of his adventures. The monks appear to have believed in his identity, and some authors assert that by the express commands of Pope Innocent the Second, a firm friend of the Emperor Lothaire the Second, he was never permitted to pass beyond the precincts of the abbey.

The historian Mezerai remarks that Henry was believed to have eventually retired to Angers, and to have ended his days as a servitor to the hospital there; having, however, previous to his death, acknowledged his rank to his confessor, and been seen and recognized by his wife Maud, daughter of Henry the Second of England, who had taken another consort in the person of Geoffrey Plantagenet of Anjou.

THE FALSE ALEXIS OF THE ORIENT.

A.D. 1186.

IN Gibbon's grand work there is, probably, no episode more graphically and characteristically described than the story of Andronicus Comnenus; and no more hapless a fate than that which the unfortunate young Emperor Alexis received at the hands of the miscreant. The whole narrative comes to us originally from the pen of the historian Nicetas, who, being Secretary of State at the time, was not only a competent recorder, but also a veritable eyewitness of many of the startling incidents he relates. Gibbon merely carries his account of the youthful monarch up to the period of his death, but Nicetas favours his readers with a record of the still more wonderful events which were associated with the name of Alexis, long after his real or alleged murder.

Upon the death of the renowned Alexis, Emperor of the Eastern Empire, his nephew, bearing the same name, was called to the throne. The young monarch being only thirteen years of age, was placed under the guardianship of his mother Xene, and of his cousin Andronicus, a man of great audacity and courage, but who, despite his royal birth, had suffered innumerable vicissitudes of fortune. Her coadjutor speedily contrived to get the empress mother banished, forcing her own son to sign the warrant of exile; and then, still fearful of the poor woman's influence in the state, had her strangled. By these criminal proceedings having got all the real power of the empire into his own hands, Andronicus determined to secure himself against the probable future competition of his nephew, whom he had already compelled to accept him as a colleague in the government, by having him murdered.

It is surprising how readily the usurper appeared to find men of high position ready to execute his nefarious schemes. Amongst the names of the five wretches who are recorded to have assassinated their youthful sovereign, is that of John Camaterus, who subsequently became Patriarch of Bulgaria, and that of a Secretary of State. Three of the murderers are said to have strangled the boy with a bowstring, and to have been subsequently assisted by two others to fling the body into the sea. After the assassination had been completed, Andronicus wished to view the body of his deceased relative, who was only fifteen at the date of his murder.

Upon the corpse being brought into his presence, the inhuman monster is recorded to have spurned it with his foot, and to have used opprobrious language to it, and of its dead parents. The head, it is averred, was then severed from the body, and, after having been mutilated and stamped with the imperial seal, was flung out of doors, whilst the rest of the poor lad's remains were enclosed in a leaden chest, and were, as above remarked, flung into the sea.

This almost incredible tale of horror is but one out of the many terrible crimes imputed to Andronicus, who amongst other deeds is alleged to have obtained forcible possession of Agnes, daughter of Louis the Seventh of France, the wife, or rather the betrothed, of the murdered Alexis. In a little while, and the cup of his enormity was full. Before the third year of his tyranny had expired the discovery of his intention to have Isaac Angelus, a person of great popularity, assassinated, drove that nobleman into open rebellion; the populace espoused his cause, placed him on the throne, and having discovered and seized Andronicus, put him to death by means of tortures too horrible to detail.

Some two years or so elapsed, during which time Isaac Angelus remained in unopposed possession of the imperial throne, when suddenly a most unexpected claimant appeared in the person of a handsome young man of about twenty years of age, who proclaimed himself to be the Emperor Alexis, supposed to have been murdered some years before. Travelling from land to land in order to obtain armed assistance for the recovery of his alleged rights, he ultimately arrived in Armenia, then under the dominion of the old Sultan Saladin. The Mohammedan sovereign was only too pleased at the prospect of a war with his Christian neighbours; he at once promised the needed assistance, asserting that it should not be said of him that he allowed so noble and accomplished a prince (who was, moreover, the son of his old friend, the Emperor Emanuel), to go wandering about the earth, despoiled of his fine empire by a relative's cruelty.

As soon as it was known that Saladin was raising troops with a view of assisting the claimant to make war upon the empire, Isaac sent an ambassador to beg him not to allow an impostor to deceive him into supporting so bad a cause. The Sultan caused the ambassador to be introduced to the pseudo Alexis, who regarded the envoy with great hauteur, and reproached him fiercely for undertaking the commission of the man who was withholding from his legitimate monarch the rights which Heaven had given him; indeed, to such an extent did his real or simulated rage carry him, that had he not been withheld he would have torn the ambassador's beard.

Whereupon Saladin stopped the interview, dismissing the ambassador with the assurance that he was resolved to support the cause of his guest unto the utmost.

Aided by the Sultan, the pretended Alexis set to work to raise troops, and, in a short time, found himself at the head of eight thousand well-equipped and determined men. He soon became the idol of his little host, which, gradually swelling by the incorporation of several bands of redoubtable warriors, speedily assumed the proportions of a regal army. Having many able officers and experienced soldiers with him, he was enabled to assume the offensive with great success, and in a short time took several cities and fortified places by assault. In Halone his victorious arms met with great resistance, which so enraged him that he put everybody to the sword, and destroyed the towns by fire. His success doubtless procured him many adherents, but there is every reason to believe numbers flocked to his banners in the belief that he was the veritable person he pretended to be; he bore a strong resemblance to the deceased prince, especially in the colour and beauty of his hair, and the hesitation or stutter in his voice.

Prince Alexis, brother of the Emperor Isaac, who commanded the army sent to oppose his progress, hesitated to give him battle, preferring stratagem to open warfare. At last a priest, who was in the service of the pretender, was suborned to relieve the imperialists of their powerful foe. Waiting his opportunity, he one night surprised his master, sleeping soundly after the day's exertions, and with his own sabre severed his head from the body. The traitor carried his ghastly spoil to the Emperor's brother, who was surprised at the remarkable resemblance which it bore to the hair and features of the unfortunate Alexis. Parting, says Nicetas, the fair locks of the severed head with his whip-handle, the imperial prince remarked that it was not without reason that several towns had received the impostor as their lawful sovereign; but, he added, "he is now punished for his crimes."

It is strange, but not unparalleled, that soon after the death of this claimant to the name and title of the young Emperor, another impostor appeared in Paphlagonia, and collected a very large number of partisans together; but after a short course of rapine and murder, he was defeated and slain by the imperial general.

THE FALSE BALDWIN OF FLANDERS.

A.D. 1225.

IN 1205 the recently elected Emperor of Constantinople, Baldwin, Hereditary Count of Flanders and Hainault, was defeated and taken prisoner by Joannice, King of Bulgaria. The release of the illustrious captive was demanded by Pope Innocent the Third, but the barbarian victor contented himself with replying that Baldwin had died in prison. He did not condescend to furnish any particulars of his decease, but rumour supplied the omission by inventing and retailing all kinds of terrible tales of his murder, the most noteworthy of which the curious reader may find upon referring to the pages of Gibbon. The real circumstances of his death never came to light, but there does not appear to be the slightest reason for doubting the fact itself; the intelligence was credited by his allies and subjects, and nothing plausible has been advanced to account for Joannice asserting it if untrue. His brother Henry, however, who, upon the news of Baldwin's defeat and capture, had been appointed Regent, would not consent to receive the imperial crown until the lapse of a twelvemonth after the fatal intelligence; and the mystery with which the barbarian victor's prisons was enshrouded would appear to have inspired the Latins with a belief in the prolonged existence of their monarch.

Be this as it may, twenty years passed away without any one appearing to question the fact of Baldwin's death. At the expiration of that period, when the sovereignty of Flanders and Hainault had devolved upon the Emperor-Count's eldest daughter Jean, a claimant appeared to assert his identity with the lost monarch. He maintained that after his capture at Adrianople he had been kindly treated by his Bulgarian captors, who, after a lapse of years, so far relaxed their watchfulness that he was enabled to effect his escape from custody; taken prisoner, however, by another barbarous tribe, unacquainted with his rank, he had been treated by them as a slave, and finally taken into Syria and sold. There for two years he had been compelled to toil as a common labourer. Enabled, by accident, to make himself known to some German merchants, who were permitted to trade in the vicinity, they had ransomed him for a small amount; and as by the death of his brother the throne of Constantinople had reverted to another, and probably hostile, branch of the family, he had deemed the recovery of his hereditary dominions an easier task than that of his Eastern empire.

The Countess Jean was at this time harassed by different feuds, domestic and foreign, and a portion of her more martially disposed subjects, wearied of female rule, received the impostor very favourably. His pretensions, however, were rejected *in toto* by the Countess, who refused to see him. Advised to have him interrogated in order to prove his imposture, she consented, and her chief counsellors had a long and wearisome interview with the pseudo monarch, who assumed a great gravity of mien and comported himself with much dignity; he paid all due observance to the questions asked him, and replied to everything with considerable plausibility. He spoke at great length, and bitterly reproached the counsellors present for not at once acknowledging him as their rightful sovereign. He was permitted uninterruptedly to address the assembly, and his words would appear to have made some impression upon the council, the president of which broke up the meeting, alleging that it would not be lawful for them to decide upon matters of such importance without learning the good will and pleasure of the Countess.

His tale now gained eager credence with the Flemings, and his claims were seconded by many noblemen, although, according to native historians, Jean had received conclusive proofs of her father's death from the hands of two envoys whom she had sent into Greece purposely to obtain information. Mezeray, the French chronicler, declares that the impostor was not only recognized by a large portion of the Flemish aristocracy, with whose genealogies, ancestors' deeds, and family names he displayed a perfect knowledge, but was also put in possession of the whole of Flanders by an enthusiastic people. To impress the populace he appeared in a scarlet garb, and carrying a white baton in his hand; and his imposture was all the more successful because of his really bearing no little resemblance to the veritable Baldwin.

Finding himself so well supported, he attempted to obtain possession of the Countess Jean, but she fled into France, and besought the protection of her cousin, Louis the Eighth, king of that country. Louis came to Compiegne, whither also, under promise of a safe conduct, came the pseudo Baldwin to meet him. The pretender was accompanied in a manner suited to his assumed rank, and upon being introduced to the king saluted him proudly. According to some annalists, Louis, after a long discourse, in which he asked the claimant to produce some document, or other authentic proof of his identity, was prompted by his counsellor, the Bishop of Beauvais, to put three test questions, which were: " Firstly, In what place he had rendered homage to Philip Augustus, King of France, for his Countship of Flanders? Secondly, By whom, and in what place, had he been invested with knighthood? Thirdly, In what place, and on what day, was he married to his wife Marguerite, daughter of the Count of Champagne?"

Taken by surprise, the impostor requested three days in order to prepare replies to these questions; and, as it was pointed out, as the lapse of twenty years might have impaired his memory, this demand was not, after all, so unreasonable. King Louis, however, found his answers so contradictory, and so generally unsatisfactory, that he commanded him to leave France within three days, not being enabled, in consequence of the safe conduct granted to him, to have him punished for his deception.

The pseudo Baldwin, being thus deprived of all hopes of the French king's aid or countenance, hastened to Valenciennes, where fresh disappointments awaited him. His allies, who from various reasons had espoused his cause, now began rapidly to desert him, and in far less time than it had taken him to attain his transient grandeur, he beheld himself divested of his borrowed plumes, and forced to fly in disguise. He attempted to get into Burgundy, where he had expectations of support, but his disguise was penetrated, his path discovered, and he himself captured by a Burgundian named Erard Castenac, who sold him to the Countess Jean for four hundred silver marks. The Countess at once adopted the prevalent method of obtaining information by putting him to the torture, and under it he is alleged to have confessed that he was Bertrand de Rans, a native of Champagne, and had been led to attempt his imposition whilst living as a hermit in a forest near Valenciennes. An old Belgian chronicle, recording his confession at full length, alleges that he had frequently heard the citizens bewailing the sad fate of Flanders in having to submit to the rule of a woman, the Countess Jean's husband being in perpetual imprisonment in France, and how they praised their late ruler Baldwin, often exclaiming, "Ah! if our dear prince could only return once more to Flanders, what a change there would be!"

Thus incited, the idea gradually formed in the Champagner's mind to personate the absent monarch, so that one day when some of these citizens were bemoaning their loss in the usual style, he startled them by exclaiming, "How do you know that your prince, after escaping from captivity, did not at once return to his country?" These words seemed to coincide with some suspicions his visitors had formed, probably from hints he had already dropped; and when they retired, although they did not dare say anything to him personally, they took good care to let everybody know what they had seen, heard, and suspected. The intelligence was rapidly disseminated all over Flanders, and was heard in all ranks, both high and low. Multitudes, including many of the higher classes, visited the hermit, and were received with an assumption of majesty that fully confirmed them in their belief. In the meanwhile Bertrand played his game so skilfully that it really appeared as if he were desirous of not being recognized as the long-lost Baldwin. At last, one day, one of his visitors had the courage or the impudence to say, "It is believed that you are Baldwin disguised in this hermit's garb;" whereupon he, thinking that the favourable opportunity for airing his pretensions had now arrived, responded sharply, "Those who imagine this do not deceive themselves, for besides me there never has been any Baldwin, Emperor of the Greeks, Count of Flanders and Hainault."

Upon hearing this declaration, all present, both high and low, saluted him as their sovereign, and furnished him with such money as they could raise; in a little while he attained to the height of his short-lived prosperity, whence, as has been seen, he as quickly fell.

After this confession had been obtained from the pretender he was condemned to death, but previously to the carrying out of the capital sentence was bound to a horse, and in that ignominious manner publicly exhibited in all the chief cities of the Netherlands. Finally he was hanged at Lille.

His execution did not dissipate the belief in the justness of his claim; the populace, says Mezeray, the French historian, preferring to believe that rather than resign her sovereignty, the Countess had had her father hanged. Matthew Paris, in his brief account of this imposture, declares that he was Baldwin, and that all his misfortunes arose from him having murdered an Eastern maiden, whom he had promised to marry and baptize; punishment overtaking him not because of the murder, but for "the uncanonical omission of baptism before its perpetration."

The Lilleois were fully confirmed in their belief of the hanged man's identity with Baldwin from the somewhat singular circumstance that after the execution the Countess Jean founded a great hospital in their city, and had placed upon everything in and about the building the bizarre design of a gibbet.

THE FALSE FREDERICK THE SECOND OF GERMANY.

A.D. 1284.

TAKE it for all in all, the case of this claimant is certainly the most wonderful one on record. For thirty-eight years Frederick the Second had nominally ruled Germany, but his foreign wars and Italian States had occupied so much of his time that only seven years of his long reign were really spent in his imperial dominions. He died at Férentino, in 1250, in the fifty-fifth year of his age; and in a little while the enormously extended empire which he had obtained for his family had passed from their hands, and his many sons, and even his grandsons, were despoiled of their crowns, and lost their lives by violence.

Warfare and contention in the various states succeeded Frederick's decease. In Germany a long interregnum of misery ensued, and it was not until 1273, when Rudolph of Hapsburgh was elected to the imperial crown, that the nation could obtain either the administration of justice or respite from hostilities, foreign and intestine. Rudolph's long reign proved very beneficial to the distracted empire, and for several years Germany enjoyed an unwonted amount of prosperity, when, in 1284, the people were startled by the report that Frederick the Second, whom for thirty-four years everybody had believed dead and buried, was still alive, and, although nearly ninety years old, seeking to recover the imperial crown.

And true it was that an aged man, claiming to be the supposed defunct monarch, had appeared, giving so plausible an account of his lengthy seclusion, and displaying so remarkable a knowledge of Frederick's most private transactions, that multitudes, including the Landgrave of Thuringia and other important personages, believed his story and afforded him support.

The narration which he gave to account for his long silence, and abstention from the exercise of his imperial functions, was as follows: Declaring himself persistently to be Frederick the Second, Emperor of Germany, King of Naples and Sicily, the old man traced the story of his life back to A.D. 1250, when, as he truly stated, the last of the Swabian emperors, worn out with his ceaseless conflicts with the Papacy, disheartened by his own reverses and the capture by the Bolognese of his illegitimate son Encius, King of Sardinia, retired to his castle of Férentino, in the Capitanate of Naples. Here, according to historical records, Frederick died of dysentery, but, according to the tale put forward by the aged claimant, no such event took place. Wearied with the world, troubled by the bane of excommunication, and sickened by the fatality which overtook his progeny one after the other, he, Frederick, determined to forsake the pomp of royalty and seek an undiscoverable retreat. Feigning illness, he sent for one of his former retainers, a man who had long since left his service, and whose brother was Prior of the Carthusian Monastery of Squillace, in Calabria. To this old servitor he communicated his purpose, and besought him to accompany his former master to this frightfully secluded place, which St. Bruno, institutor of the Carthusian Monks, had founded. He consented to Frederick's wish. A very faithful valet, by the Emperor's order, now set to work to disinter the body of a man of about fifty years of age, who, conveniently for the purpose, had died the preceding day, and had, in accordance with southern custom, been buried a few hours after his death. Luckily for the success of the scheme, the night was very obscure, so that the man was enabled unobserved to bring his ghastly burden under the Emperor's window, where, by means of a rope, the confederates succeeded in drawing it up into the chamber. The dead body was dressed in the Emperor's attire and placed in the imperial bed, whereupon Frederick and his follower descended by the rope into the garden, and, quite unnoticed by the guards, made good their retreat.

By easy stages the Chartreuse was reached, and the Emperor, after rewarding the Sicilian valet with diamonds of sufficient value to keep him in comfort for the rest of his days, made rich offerings to the Prior, and then, without revealing his real name or condition, was received into the monastery as a simple brother, and as such was employed in the cultivation of the adjacent garden.

In this healthy occupation, ran the pretender's story, he continued until 1268, when his unfortunate young grandson Conradrin was atrociously beheaded by order of Charles of Anjou. He then changed his abode to another Carthusian monastery in Champagne, near the town of Luni, and thence he passed into Germany once more, and as all his male descendants were deceased, asserted his right to reclaim the imperial crown.

Many persons believed, or appeared to believe, this strange story. The Landgrave of Thuringia, and others of less note, publicly proffered their allegiance. The people of West Friesland, then at war with Florentius, Count of Holland, sent deputies to him to complain of the perpetual raids which the

Dutch made into their lands, and to beg him to protect them as vassals of the empire against the insults and vexations of their enemies. The pseudo Frederick, only too glad of the opportunity of airing his pretensions, wrote to Count Florentius to the effect that unless he at once desisted from this warfare, he would put him under the ban of the empire, and attack him with the imperial forces; moreover, if he had, as he asserted, any right to Friesland, let him come to him, Frederick, at Misina, to produce his evidence and receive the Imperial decision.

The Count of Holland was greatly enraged at this affront, but, as recorded by Vossius in his History of Holland, condescended to reply, to the effect that his correspondent had plenty of assurance to take upon himself the name of the Emperor Frederick the Second, thirty-four years after that monarch's death. There were, however, he reminded the claimant, yet living persons who had beheld Frederick's dead body; whilst, as he pointed out, not only were the Emperor's affairs at the time of his death far from desperate enough to cause him to conceal himself, but also the impossibility for such an illustrious personage to have remained for so long a time in obscurity. He then strongly advised the pretender to quietly return to his proper station in society, adding that he could not have any dread of his armaments, seeing that he possessed none, not even being master of Misina, where he resided.

Not satisfied with this exhibition of his claims, the pseudo Frederick now wrote to the Emperor Rudolph commanding him to resign the imperial dignity, and unattended, and simply as a tributary prince, to come and do homage to him, his sovereign. This was too much for the patience of Rudolph, who soon determined to dispose of this competitor for his crown. Historians differ somewhat as to how he obtained possession of the claimant, but according to the most reliable accounts he would appear to have been taken prisoner at Wetzlaer, in Hesse, after that town had sustained a cruel siege on his account; thence he was taken to Nuz, in the Electorate of Cologne, and, after having been subjected to torture, confessed, so it was declared, that his real name was Tilon Colup, and that the many private details of Frederick's life, of which he had displayed such an intimate knowledge, were learnt whilst he was in the Emperor's service as a domestic. Contemporary records aver that he bore great resemblance to Frederick, that he was perfectly acquainted with the most minute particulars of that monarch's life, both public and private, and that he simulated the deceased sovereign so well in conversation that he convinced all with whom he conversed.

Ultimately, he was sentenced to death as a necromancer, and, together with two of his chief adherents, burnt to death in Nuz. The inhabitants of Colmar, a large town in the hereditary dominions of Frederick, who had embraced the claimant's cause with great zeal, were inflicted with a heavy pecuniary fine in lieu of death, to which punishment they were, at first, sentenced.

THE FALSE VOLDEMAR THE SECOND OF BRANDENBURG.

A.D. 1345-54.

THE history of this adventurer is rendered more than usually interesting from the fact that several authors have taken up cudgels on his behalf, and vehemently assert that he was truly the man he asserted himself to be. Not only authors' ink, but, unfortunately, a great quantity of human blood was wasted in the dispute, and that, too, without the world being any the wiser. The facts, as they are recounted by historians, stand thus:

Voldemar the Second, Marquis of Brandenburg, was the thirteenth Elector of the family of the Counts of Ascagne, a family closely related to many of the royal houses of Europe. After a reign of about three years, Voldemar, following the example of so many of his contemporaries, determined upon making a pilgrimage to the Holy Land. Having settled all his temporal affairs, and left his brother, John the Fourth, in possession of his electorate, he started upon his pilgrimage, attended only by two men.

He set off on his journey without informing his brother, or any of his subjects, what route he intended taking, or, indeed, furnishing information of any kind relative to his intentions.

Voldemar and his brother John were the only surviving members of the elder branch of the House of Ascagne; but, previous to his departure, the royal pilgrim obliged his subjects to swear that, in the event of him and his brother dying childless, they would receive for their sovereign a prince of the House of Anhalt, which was a branch of the Ascagne family. This was A.D. 1320.

Twenty-four days after Voldemar's departure his brother John died suddenly, not without suspicion that he had been poisoned. The absent Elector, apparently unconscious of the sad event, did not return, and, it was quickly noised abroad, had also met with a sudden death.

The Emperor Louis, acting in opposition to all right, save that of might, instead of allowing the duly recognized prince to succeed, took possession of the electorate, and invested his own son Louis with it. This usurpation would appear to have been effected without exciting much opposition at the time, but, eventually, after numberless declarations and reservations of their rights had been made by different princes of the empire, the whole question was reopened by the appearance of a man claiming to be the long-lost Voldemar. In order to afford a fair idea of this pretender's claims, it will be necessary in the first place to recount the story of his appearance as detailed by the authors favouring the theory of his being an impostor, and then to produce the evidence offered by those of the opposite party on his behalf.

The received opinion is that Rudolph, Duke and Elector of Saxony, being desirous of wresting the Electorate of Brandenburg from Louis of Bavaria, the Emperor's son, under the pretence that he himself was a member of the House of Ascagne, and finding it difficult to get the two electorates (of Saxony and Brandenburg) vested in one person, produced a certain man, whom he doubtless meant to use as a tool. This man he declared to be his dear cousin Voldemar, who had disappeared nearly twenty-five years previously, on a pilgrimage to the chief places of the Holy Land; which he had, it was given forth, visited, but had been taken prisoner and been kept in captivity by the infidels until recently, when he had contrived to effect his escape.

Several different versions of this story exist; some writers assert that the pseudo Voldemar was a miller of Sandreslaw, and others say a native of Beltztize, named Jacques Reboc; he was, they moreover allege, an habitual liar, and a cunning vagabond, possessing some resemblance, in form and face, to the lost prince; such resemblance, indeed, as the number of years that had elapsed since his disappearance, combined with the fatigues and miseries he had endured, might have left in the veritable Voldemar. He had, they add, dwelt for a number of years in Saxony, where he had been well instructed as to the former life and family connections of the deceased Elector, as well as put in the way of counterfeiting on his person the various marks by which he might deceive the world.

Thus runs the story as told by the advocates for the imposture theory; presently it will be seen what can be said on the other side; whilst now it will be as well to hear what happened upon the appearance of the claimant. The rumour of Voldemar's return from a long and painful captivity in Turkey having quickly spread over Germany, the people were everywhere in a state of intense excitement to see him; and when he reached Brandenburg, the populace at once declared for him, and compelled the Elector Louis to retire. Charles the Fourth, who had succeeded Louis the Fourth as emperor, and was on bad terms with the Elector Louis, the late monarch's son, declared for the claimant, as did also the rulers of Brunswick, Pomerania, Mecklenburg, and several others, including Voldemar's relatives, the Duke of Saxony and the Princes of Anhalt.

In 1348, a Congress was held, at which almost all the nobility recognized the claimant as the legitimate Elector; whilst, as for the lower classes, they received him back with transports of joy; such was their enthusiasm at getting their old ruler back, indeed, and their delight at being delivered from the dominion of the Bavarians, who had taken possession of their country after it had been for two hundred years governed by the House of Ascagne, that they furnished the supposed Voldemar bountifully with goods and money, and rendered him every assistance towards driving out Louis. Almost all the towns and cities acknowledged his authority, and promised obedience to his rule.

Louis at once commenced proceedings for the recovery of his lost electorate; aided by Casimir, King of Poland, the King of Denmark, who singularly enough was also named Voldemar, and by some other potentates equally desirous of having a hand in their neighbour's affairs, he soon found himself able to place a good army in the field. A desultory warfare, that endured for some years, now commenced between the rival electors, but finally Voldemar inflicted such a signal defeat upon his opponent's forces that Louis relinquished the contest in disgust, and retired to his domains in the Tyrol, making over his claim upon Brandenburg to his two younger brothers. This transference of the electorate, it should be mentioned, the Emperor Charles afterwards confirmed by letters patent in 1350, notwithstanding the contestation of Voldemar and his partisans.

According to the popular account, the pseudo Voldemar was ultimately overthrown, condemned to death, and burnt as an impostor; whilst the veritable Marquis is stated to have died in 1322, either at a place called Korekei, or at Stendell.

Thus runs the commonly accredited story; but summing up later and equally reliable records, the favourers of the idea that it was really the Elector himself who reappeared put the case thus. The Archbishop of Magdeburg, Primate of Germany, a man totally uninterested either way, and known for his probity, would not, they say, have recognised and have given his testimony on behalf of the claimant unless satisfied as to his identity; nor, they further remark, would the Emperor Charles and so many other princes have exposed their lives and caused the effusion of so much human blood for an impostor.

Moreover, one historian shows from contemporary records that by the Electoral College of Germany

Voldemar was still believed to be alive in 1338, sixteen years after his alleged death; but as the official letter is only founded on a belief, its citation is worthless. The statement as to his decease in 1322 is, they point out, contradictory, whilst had the Elector Louis known of his predecessor's death, why did he not procure documentary evidence of the same? The Emperor Louis was known, moreover, to have entertained great hatred against the House of Ascagne, in consequence of its chiefs, Rudolph of Saxony and Voldemar the First, uncle of the second Voldemar, having declared for his rival for the empire, Frederick of Austria, in 1313.

What, however, chiefly confirms their view of the case in the eyes of the claimant's advocates is, not only did Voldemar's relatives, the Duke of Saxony and the Princes of Anhalt, and that apparently contrary to their interest, acknowledge the wanderer, but they even, when he died at Dessau, in 1354, nine years after his return, laid his bones amongst those of the ancestors of their illustrious house. According to the chronicle of Magdeburg, he was buried at Dessau in the Chapel du Saint Esprit, which was the general place of sepulture for the princes of the sovereign house of Anhalt.

THE FALSE RICHARD THE SECOND OF ENGLAND.

A.D. 1404.

ENGLISH history, unfortunately, furnishes several examples of royal claimants, whose pretensions have but too frequently caused great effusion of blood. One of the earliest of these cases occurred soon after the mysterious disappearance of Richard the Second from Pontefract Castle. How the king died, and by what means, is an unfathomable secret; but there is little reason for doubting that he was murdered by the adherents of Henry the Fourth. Many favoured the idea, however, that he had escaped from the hands of his jailers and had reached a place of safety. "It is most strange," remarks the old chronicler, Speed, "that King Richard was not suffered to be dead after he had so long a time been buried."

For some years rumours of the king being still alive and in Scotland were industriously circulated all over the country, and believed in by many; so that in 1404, when Warde, a Court jester, who much resembled the deceased monarch, was induced by a gentleman named Serle, or Serlo, to personate him, numbers, including some titled personages, were deceived into deeming that Richard was still alive.

The late king's privy seal was counterfeited, and letters despatched to many of his old adherents to assure them of his being alive, and of his intention to shortly show himself in England again. These 'forged impositions" produced the desired effect upon many, including the old Countess of Oxford, who either credited or pretended to credit the intelligence, and distributed a number of gold and silver harts, such as Richard was accustomed to give his followers, to be worn as cognizances.

Henry soon heard of these proceedings, and Serle's messenger being arrested, gave up the names of the parties with whom he communicated. Several monks were arrested; the old Countess was imprisoned; and her private secretary, who had repeatedly affirmed that he had spoken with King Richard, was barbarously executed. Serle was soon afterwards betrayed into Henry's hands, and is declared to have confessed everything connected wth the conspiracy. He was drawn on a sledge through all the principal towns from Pontefract to London, and executed at the latter place as a traitor. The alleged originator of the scheme and his abettors having been thus disposed of, the whole affair would appear to have been speedily forgotten.

THE FALSE MUSTAPHA OF TURKEY.

A.D. 1425.

BAJARET THE FIRST, surnamed *Yilderim*, or "The Lightning," from his impetuosity, after a long, uninterrupted career of victory, during which he had held all Europe at bay, in a single battle in 1402 succumbed to the irresistible power of Timur the Great, losing everything but life. Amongst those who fell in the almost unprecedented carnage of this terrible field was, it is supposed, Mustapha, the Turkish Sultan's eldest son and heir.

In 1403 Bajaret died, or, according to another authority, brained himself against the iron bars of the cage in which his conqueror is stated to have retained him. The remaining sons of the deceased monarch contrived to elude the vigilance of Tamerlane, and at once commenced fighting amongst themselves. For eleven years they kept the tottering empire in a chronic state of intestine warfare, but finally, Mohammed, the youngest, obtained the reins of power, and speedily reinstated the nation in its former glory. In 1422, after a short but successful reign, Mohammed the First died, and was succeeded by his son, Amurath the Second, who had just attained his eighteenth year.

Up to 1421 no one would appear to have entertained any doubt of the death of Prince Mustapha at the famous battle of Angora, when suddenly he, or a claimant to his name, appeared, and demanded the sovereignty of the empire, by virtue of being Bajaret's eldest son. Who this man was still remains doubtful. With the single exception of Nectori, who is, however, a creditable authority, all the Turkish historians declare this *soi disant* Mustapha to have been an impostor, whilst Christian writers, favouring the Greek cause, persistently assert him to have been the veritable prince himself.

Be the pretender who he may, no sooner did he emerge from obscurity than he obtained allies and adherents only too willing to share in the promised plunder of an empire. Joined by the Prince of Walachia, and by Djouneïd, Governor of Nicopolis, whom the too generous Sultan Mohammed had already twice pardoned for rebellion, the claimant invaded Thessaly. Defeated and put to flight in the neighbourhood of Salonica, he took refuge in that city, putting himself under the protection of the Greek commandant, who justified his confidence by refusing to give him up to the vengeance of his conquerors. The Emperor Emanuel highly approved of the commandant's conduct, and to the request of his powerful neighbour, the Sultan, that he should surrender the fugitive, responded that no monarch could act so shamelessly as to deliver up a prince who sought an asylum at the foot of his throne. He promised, however, that during the lifetime of Mohammed, the *soi disant* Mustapha should not be permitted to leave the Greek court. The Sultan contented himself with this promise of the Emperor, and agreed to pay a pension of three hundred thousand *astres** to the pretender; thus, it has been pointed out, tacitly recognizing him as of the royal blood. The Governor Djouneïd and thirty of his companions were included in the treaty of pardon, but Mohammed invaded and ravaged the dominions of the Prince of Walachia, in revenge for the aid he had afforded the rebels.

The following year Mohammed the First was struck with apoplexy, and died suddenly, leaving his empire, as before stated, to his son, Amurath the Second. The new ruler immediately advised the neighbouring princes of his accession to the Turkish throne, entering into alliances, and making truces or treaties of peace with such as had been hostile to the Ottoman power. All but the Greek Emperor appeared to be friendlily disposed, and he, doubtless

* A Turkish coin value half-a-crown.

thinking to take advantage of the new monarch's youth, instantly summoned Amurath to place his brothers in his hands, as hostages for the performance of some clause in his father's testament. Emanuel, moreover, threatened the youthful Sultan that unless he complied with the demand, he would release Mustapha, his uncle, the legitimate heir to the Turkish throne, and assist him by force of arms to recover his usurped rights.

Amurath's clever minister refused the demand with indignation, asserting that the law of the prophet did not permit the children of true believers to be brought up amongst *ghiaours*.* The Greek Emperor, true to his menace, and all unmindful of the dangerous vicinity of the Ottoman dominions to his own, set the pretender free, and gave him every requisite for the commencement of his dangerous adventure, upon condition that he made over Gallipoli, and several other towns, to the Greeks.

Thus befriended, the royal claimant, accompanied by ten galleys containing his followers and adherents, proceeded to Gallipoli, where he no sooner disembarked than the town and suburbs acknowledged his pretensions, only the garrison of the fortress holding out. Leaving a small besieging force before the town, he made rapid marches towards the Isthmus

* Infidels; literally, dogs.

of Athos, his army increasing rapidly as he proceeded, and several places falling into his hands. The Sultan sent his Vizier to Adrianople, where he collected an army of thirty thousand men, with which to oppose the invaders. Several great vassals of the empire having now declared for Mustapha, he was quite prepared to face the imperial army, and as soon as it came in view he advanced courageously towards it, and commanded the troops to lay down their arms. As if by magic, says one historian, the soldiers obeyed, and the pretender suddenly found himself master of the situation without having to lose a single man. The unfortunate Vizier and his brother were captured; the former was put to death, but the latter released.

On receipt of this intelligence the fortress of Gallipoli capitulated, and Demetrius, the commander of the Greek forces, was about to garrison it with his soldiers when Mustapha interposed, and, unmindful of his treaty with Emanuel, said that he was not making war for the Emperor's profit. The Greeks, thus beholding all their hopes of aggrandizement dissipated, sought to renew their alliance with the Sultan, but their monarch obstinately persisting in his demand for Amurath's brothers being placed in his hands as hostages, the negotiations fell through.

As soon as the Ottoman sovereign learnt the

defection of his army, he energetically set to work to collect another, and to obtain the aid of surrounding nations. Encouraged by the promise of victory given him by the saintly Emir of Bokhara, he proceeded with his hastily improvised forces to meet the rebels, ultimately taking up a strong position behind the river Ouloubad. Mustapha, on his side, was advancing quickly to give battle, when he was suddenly seized with a violent bleeding at the nose, which weakened him so much that for three days he was compelled to suspend the attack. The delay was fatal to him. Taking advantage of the respite, emissaries of Amurath penetrated into the hostile ranks, and persuaded large numbers of soldiers and officers to return to their former master, whilst the Arabs, who remained faithful to Mustapha, having attempted to surprise the imperial troops, were cut into pieces by the Janissaries. Djouneïd, the thrice-dyed traitor, seeing how matters were going, still further injured the pretender's cause by passing over to the enemy with all his followers. Believing themselves abandoned by their chiefs, the soldiers fled in all directions in disorder, leaving their unfortunate leader in the company of a few servants. He took refuge in Gallipoli, but seeing the fleet of his fortunate rival approaching to besiege the place, he resumed his flight, and took shelter in Walachia.

Betrayed, however, by some of his personal attendants, he was seized, taken to Adrianople, and put to death, having been hanged, according to some accounts, from the battlements of the city walls.

When the defeat and death of Mustapha was communicated to the Greek Emperor, he began to fear for himself. He despatched ambassadors to the Sultan to make protestations of his friendship, and to leave no stone unturned to avert his wrath. His efforts were useless: at the head of twenty thousand men, Amurath, aided by a Genoese fleet, crossed over to Europe, and advancing to the walls of Constantinople, besieged Emanuel in his capital. Encouraged by the presence and prophecies of the Emir of Bokhara, the Mussulmans were impatient for the assault on the world-famed city. After long meditations, the holy man solemnly proclaimed that at one hour after midday of the 24th of August, 1422, he should mount his steed, and thrice waving his scimitar, and thrice giving the war-cry of " Allah and his prophet," the Mohammedans were to advance, and the city would be theirs.

Accordingly, on the day and the hour promised, the Emir, mounted on a magnificent charger, and escorted by five hundred dervishes, advancing towards the beleaguered city, gave the anticipated signal; his words were caught up and thrice repeated by the whole invading army. Uttering defiant war-cries, the Greek soldiery advanced, and in a short time both armies were hotly engaged. And now was beheld one of the most wonderful phenomena recorded in the annals of nations, but which is, unfortunately, so differently stated by the Christian and Mohammedan chroniclers, that it is difficult to reconcile the two versions; the better way will be, doubtless, to believe neither.

The sun was sinking below the horizon, without victory having declared for either side, when suddenly, say the favourers of the Greek version, in the midst of the golden rays of the setting luminary was beheld a virgin, clothed in a violet robe, and blinding the eyes of the besiegers with the supernatural glare which surrounded her. Panic stricken, the Mohammedans fled, and Constantinople was saved; saved, the Christians asserted, by the Virgin Mary herself.

As might be expected, the story told by the Mussulmans was very different, the miracle, if they are to be believed, having been performed on their behalf, and their withdrawal from before the city having been caused by a totally different occurrence. Their retreat, indeed, was the result of the Emperor Emanuel's policy. Seeing all his plans frustrated by the pretender's death, he hit upon the idea of resuscitating him. Having obtained a man to suit his purpose, another Mustapha was started, fresh revolts excited, and Amurath compelled to raise the siege of the imperial city, in order to make use of his army to put down the new aspirant to his throne.

The second *soi disant* Mustapha did not enjoy his borrowed plumes for long: some towns, it is true, succumbed to him, and others bought his forbearance, but no sooner had he got within reach of the hostile army than Elias, a man who had urged him to undertake the imposture, seduced by the Sultan's gold, betrayed him to Amurath, and he was executed on the field of battle.

THE FALSE EDWARD THE SIXTH OF ENGLAND.

A.D. 1486.

THE frequency, in the middle ages, with which sovereigns and members of royal families met with mysterious deaths afforded full scope for the ingenious to exercise their talents in assuming the names and titles of deceased princes. As the murderers, or those who profited by the murder, often could not conveniently produce proofs of the absent person's decease, the claimant was frequently enabled to make good use of his rival's reticence; but, almost invariably, even if the fraud were not discovered, the pretender was overthrown, and nearly always paid for his temerity by an ignominious or, at all events, a violent death. The subject of the present sketch is almost the only impostor, proved to be one, who met with a luckier fate.

The manner in which Richard the Third disposed of his nephews, Edward the Fifth and Richard, Duke of York, was so mysterious and secret, that it is not strange that it gave rise to many curious complications, the perplexities of which had to be suffered by his successor. Presuming the two young princes to have been put to death, the next *male* heir to the throne, upon the demise of Richard the Third, was Edward, Earl of Warwick, the son of the late Duke of Clarence. At one time, indeed, Richard had treated the boy as heir-apparent, but his jealousy becoming aroused, he had him detained as a prisoner in the manor-house of Sheriff Hutton, doubtless with a view of causing him to share ultimately the sad fate of his cousins. One of the earliest acts of Henry the Seventh, after the defeat and death of Richard at Bosworth Field, was to secure the person of the Earl of Warwick; he had the youthful captive brought up to London, from Yorkshire, and then the poor boy, "born to perpetual calamity," as Hall remarks, "was incontinent in the Tower of London put under safe and sure custody."

The place of this unfortunate prince's durance, Henry's known character, and the apparently parallel case of his two cousins, quickly gave rise to the rumour that Edward had died suddenly. This intelligence corresponded with the projected schemes of a certain Richard Simon, a priest residing at Oxford. This man for some time past, if Bacon and other authorities are to be believed, had been educating a baker's son, Lambert Simnel by name, to play a daring and apparently hopeless part in his ambitious game, and the news of the Earl of Warwick's death afforded him the desired opportunity of taking the first step. The priest and his pupil, a lad of no small natural dignity and tact, proceeded to Ireland,. and in November, 1486, landed at Dublin.

Simon introduced his pupil to the Earl of Kildare first, and finding him only too willing to accept his story, openly proclaimed the boy to be Edward, son of the Duke of Clarence, escaped from his imprisonment in the Tower. The nobles and gentry in Ireland crowded to see the pseudo prince, who is recorded to have been "not only beautiful and graceful in person, but witty and ingenious. He told his touching story with great consistency, and, when questioned, he could give minute particulars relating to the royal family." The Earl of Kildare, who was Lord Lieutenant, or Deputy of Ireland, presented Simon's *protégé* to the people "as sole male heir left of the line of Richard, Duke of York," and consequently the rightful ruler of that realm. A large number of Irish hereupon acknowledged him as their monarch; the citizens of Dublin declaring unanimously in his favour; "so that," says Bacon, "with marvellous consent and applause, this counterfeit Plantagenet was brought with great solemnity to the castle of Dublin, and there saluted, served, and honoured as king; the boy becoming it well, and doing nothing that did betray the baseness of his condition."

Messengers were sent into England and Flanders for assistance, in the meanwhile that the boy was solemnly crowned and anointed in the cathedral of Dublin, by the Bishop of Meath, as Edward the Sixth, under which name he issued writs, convoked a parliament, and performed other acts of legal authority, without there being a single sword drawn in King Henry's favour.

When intelligence of this affair reached Henry's ears, he at once summoned a council to meet at the Charterhouse, near Shene, and the result of their deliberations was that Edward Plantagenet should be taken out of the Tower, and publicly shown to the citizens, to prove the levity and imposture of the proceedings in Ireland; secondly, that a general pardon or amnesty should be granted "to all that would reveal their offences, and submit themselves by a certain day," and this pardon was to be so ample that not even high treason—" no, not against the King's own person"—should be excepted. Lastly, it was resolved the Queen Dowager, Henry's mother-in-law, should be arrested, imprisoned, and *her goods confiscated*, under the absurd pretence that she had broken her agreement with Henry in delivering her daughters out of sanctuary into the late King Richard's hands. This last resolution every one could readily perceive was adopted from a motive different to the alleged one, and Bacon hints that Henry suspected his royal relative of having prompted, to suit her own purposes, the priest and his *protégé* Lambert in their undertaking. Whatever the cause of her imprisonment, the King, says the historian, sustained great obloquy for it, " which, nevertheless, was somewhat sweetened to him by a great confiscation."

The pardon was accordingly proclaimed; the Queen-mother imprisoned in the nunnery of Bermondsey; and the unfortunate veritable Prince Edward was brought forth from his imprisonment in the Tower, and on a Sunday taken through the principal streets to St. Paul's Cathedral, where a large number of persons had congregated; " and it was provided also in good fashion, that divers of the nobility and others of quality (especially of those that the King most suspected and knew the person of Plantagenet best), had communication with the young gentleman by the way." The poor lad was then re-conducted to his place of durance, after having, so far as England was concerned, served his jailer's purpose. The Irish, however, had gone too far to be disconcerted by this exhibition, and they loudly declared that it was Henry who had "tricked up a boy in the likeness of Edward Plantagenet, and showed him to the people," to suit his own plans.

At this time, also, unexpected succour arrived in Ireland for the pretender. John de la Pole, Earl of Lincoln, nephew of the two late kings, Edward the Fourth and Richard the Third, and, after Edward Plantagenet, the legitimate heir to the Yorkist claims, had fled from the clutches of Henry the Seventh to the protection of his aunt, Margaret of Burgundy. The Duchess, ever ready to assist the Yorkist cause, had at once entered into the Simnel plot, and promised all the aid in her power. She fitted out a regiment of two thousand mercenaries, put them under the command of Martin Swartz, a skilled veteran, and sent them with the Earl of Lincoln into Ireland. Thus assisted, the Irish malcontents insisted upon being led into England, and, despite the more prudent advice of some of their council, this plan was adopted. Under the leadership of the Earls of Lincoln and Kildare, the pretender and his adherents crossed over to Lanarkshire, where they were joined by a small body of English under Sir Thomas Broughton.

Henry, meanwhile, lost no time in raising troops, and by the time the rebels had reached Stoke, near

Newark, they came into contact with the King's army. The battle was obstinately contested, but the pretender's small and ill-armed forces had no chance against the royal troops. " Martin Swartz, with his Germans, performed bravely, and so did those few English that were on that side; neither did the Irish fail in courage or fierceness, but being almost naked men, only armed with darts and skeans, it was rather an execution than a fight upon them; insomuch as the furious slaughter of them was a great discouragement and appalment to the rest." The German veterans died in their ranks almost to a man, and the rebels did not succumb until one-half of their number, including nearly all their leaders, had fallen on the field; while some hundreds of the royalists perished. Amongst the slain were the Earls of Lincoln and Kildare, Sir Thomas Broughton, Colonel Swartz, and, it is presumed, Lord Lovel; whilst amongst the prisoners were the pseudo king, and his tutor, Richard Simon.

As soon as the pretender was proved to be only plain Lambert Simnel, Henry took him into his service, and employed him in the royal kitchen as a turnspit; ultimately promoting him to be one of the King's falconers,—" Henry," says Bacon, " out of wisdom, thinking that if he suffered death he would be forgotten too soon; but being kept alive he would be a continual spectacle, and a kind of remedy against the like enchantments of people in time to come." As for the priest, observes this same authority, "he was committed close prisoner, and heard of no more; *the King loving to seal up his own dangers.*"

THE FALSE RICHARD THE FOURTH OF ENGLAND.

A.D. 1491-99.

THE fate of the leading conspirators in Lambert Simnel's case, instead of acting as a warning to deter others from similar attacks, really appeared as if it were only designed as prelude to a far more serious attempt to wrest the crown from Henry's head. Unfortunately for the welfare of England, no sooner had the pseudo Edward been disposed of, than the King had to contend with another and a far more redoubtable claimant to the throne.

In 1491 this new aspirant to the crown began to noise his pretensions abroad, proclaiming himself to be Richard, the younger of the two sons of the deceased King Edward, who were supposed to have been murdered in the Tower by order of their uncle, the late King Richard the Third. This young claimant, admitted to have been a youth of noble aspect, and in features much resembling the late Edward the Fourth, whilst acknowledging that his elder brother had been killed, asserted that he had been permitted to escape. In a letter, which is now in the British Museum, and which the youth wrote to Isabella of Spain, he states that at the time his brother was murdered he was nine years of age; that he was sent out of England secretly, in the custody of two persons, and was compelled to take an oath that he would not divulge his name and rank to any one until after a certain number of years. Having fulfilled the conditions of his promise, he left Portugal, where he had resided for some time, and in 1492 landed in Ireland. The citizens of Cork, which was the first city he honoured with a visit, undeterred by the exposure of the late pretender to royalty, were for warmly espousing the cause of this claimant, yet were somewhat restrained by the prudence of the new Earl of Kildare. At this critical moment Charles, King of France, being at war with Henry the Seventh, sent a cordial invitation to the *soi disant* prince to come to Paris. The invitation was readily accepted, and the pretender once more crossed the seas. In France he was received everywhere with royal honours, and treated by everybody as the Duke of York, heir to the English crown. This courtesy was, however, as Bacon points out, doubtless only trickery on the part of the French king in order to force Henry into a peace. A treaty was speedily concluded between the two monarchs, one result of which was the dismissal of the young adventurer, King Charles refusing, nevertheless, to deliver up his youthful guest to the English king's untender mercies.

Forced to forsake France, the pretender betook himself to the Court of Burgundy, where the old Duchess, whose nephew he claimed to be, protected and assisted all adherents of the House of York. The old Duchess Margaret, sister of Edward the Fourth, had long asserted her belief in the existence of one of her nephews, and was only too likely to acknowledge any presentable claimant; but the support which she had rendered Simnel in his recent exploit did not tell in favour of her present *protégé*. Upon this occasion she was, or pretended to be, very searching in her scrutiny into the adventurer's story, but, at last, appearing to be perfectly convinced of the justice of his claims to kinship, she recognized him as her nephew; embraced him affectionately; styled him "The White Rose of England;" appointed him a guard of thirty persons, and furnished him with everything suitable for the maintenance of his presumed princely rank. The lad, indeed, is universally admitted to have displayed in all his conduct a noble bearing, and if he were, as Henry's partisans assert, only a wandering trader's son, he certainly did credit to the alleged secret instructions of his putative aunt.

Lord Verulam, to account for the likeness between the young pretender and the late King Edward, as also to explain his courtly bearing and princely deportment, tells a strange and extremely improbable story, to the effect that the lad was son of a converted Jew, named variously John, and Peter, Osbeck, a resident of Tournay, but whom business brought to London. This Osbeck resided in London for some time, having with him his wife, who, during the period of their residence in the English metropolis, was confined of a boy. Osbeck, says Bacon, "being known in Court, the King, either out of a religious nobleness, because he" (the father) "was a convert, or upon some private acquaintance, did him the honour to be godfather to his child," and, it is to be presumed, endowed him with regal inclinations. This needless legend is set in contrast with another in the next page, wherein the chronicler, forgetting the "religious nobleness" of the licentious monarch, subjoins that it was said, "King Edward the Fourth was his godfather, which, as it is somewhat suspicious for a wanton prince to become gossip in so mean a house, and might make a man think that he might indeed have in him some base blood of the House of York, so at the least it might give occasion to the boy, in being called 'King Edward's godson,' or, perhaps in sport, 'King Edward's son,' to entertain such thoughts in his head. For tutor he had none (for aught that appears), as Lambert Simnel had, until he came unto the Lady Margaret, who instructed him."

The advocate for the crafty, avaricious, old Tudor king, next indulges in a lengthy and apparently imaginative account of the secret tuition of the comely lad by the Duchess of Burgundy, with whose innermost thoughts Bacon professes the closest acquaintanceship. He shrewdly guesses that "Perkin Warbeck" had counterfeited for so long a time the person of the murdered prince, that at last, "with oft telling a lie, he was turned by habit almost into the thing he seemed to be, and from a liar to a believer." Be this as it may, the *soi disant* Richard, comfortably installed at the Court of Flanders, speedily discovered means of opening communications with England. Many members of the highest families, including, so it was alleged, Sir William Stanley, a relative of the King, and who had even saved Henry's life and crown at Bosworth, were involved in a plot, having for its object the overthrow of the reigning monarch, and, apparently, the substitution for him of the Burgundian *protégé*. Henry was well provided with spies, who kept him closely informed of all that was brewing; but his efforts to obtain possession of "le garson," as he termed the claimant, were unavailable; whilst all his declarations that he was perfectly at his ease with respect to the "impostor, as every one knew who and what he was," only served to display his anxiety.

By means of the King's gold, the whole of the conspiracy on foot was revealed: Sir Robert Clifford, one of the conspirators, betrayed his companions for five hundred pounds and a free pardon, and two other accomplices for sums proportionate to their lower rank. The whole details of the plot were unravelled, and the chief members of it, including Stanley, were brought to the block. Stanley's complicity in the "Perkin Warbeck" conspiracy has been doubted by modern historians, who have not hesitated to aver that his wealth was his principal crime in the King's eyes; indeed, the only charge that was made against him was, that if he were sure the claimant was King Edward's son, he would not bear arms against him.

The discovery of the plot, and the fate of its principal concocters, appeared to be a death-blow to the young adventurer's cause; but he, all undaunted, taking advantage of Henry's absence in the north, with the aid of the Duchess of Burgundy fitted out an expedition, and tried to effect a rising in England. Some portion of his followers landed at Deal, but instead of obtaining assistance were attacked by the

Kentish men, and either killed at once or made prisoners, and subsequently hanged. Discouraged by this hostile reception, "Perkin" returned to Flanders, whence he shortly betook himself once more to Ireland. There he again failed to arouse the populace on his behalf, although joined by Desmond and some others of less note. "As," says Bacon, "there was nothing left for Perkin but the blustering affection of wild and naked people," and as he had lost three of his vessels in a futile attempt to capture Waterford, he had to relinquish his efforts in that quarter.

Again repelled in his efforts to obtain a footing in Ireland, the intrepid wanderer crossed over to Scotland, to the warlike monarch of which country he carried recommendatory letters not only from the Duchess of Burgundy, but also from the French King and the Emperor of Germany. By the Scottish King the presumed prince was received with open arms, and in every way treated as if he were the personage he claimed to be. There is every reason for believing that James credited his guest's story; outwardly, at least, he paid him all deference; addressed him as "cousin," and gave him for wife his own relative, the beautiful Lady Catherine Gordon daughter of the Earl of Huntley, and granddaughter of James the First of Scotland. It seems very unlikely that the Scottish monarch would have sanctioned the marriage of Lady Catherine with the adventurer unless convinced of his royal birth.

Under the pretext of assisting his youthful guest to regain his dominions, James headed two warlike incursions into England. Unable to resist so good an opportunity of looting, the Scottish army carried off everything of value; and when the young adventurer, according to Polydore Vergil, the historian, "feigning" to be distressed at the devastation inflicted, implored the King to spare his miserable subjects, James replied, sneeringly, that it was very generous to be so careful of what did not belong to him, as not a man had yet joined his standard. No one, indeed, of any consequence did join the claimant upon these occasions; and as the raids proved disastrous to the Scottish forces, Henry was enabled to make peace on his own terms with James; offered him his eldest daughter, Margaret, in marriage, and forced him to withdraw his protection from Perkin.

Compelled once more to resume his search for an asylum, the luckless pretender, accompanied by his beautiful wife and a few faithful followers, left Scotland; not, however, without bearing away with him some substantial proof of the Scottish King's regard. Again he sought shelter in Ireland, but the Irish appearing less disposed than before to espouse his cause, he departed for Cornwall, where much discontent prevailed on account of Henry's oppressive taxation. With only three vessels and seventy men the claimant landed at Whitsand Bay, near Land's End, on the 7th September, 1497. He sent his wife to St. Michael's Mount for safety; and then, at the head of an irregular body of three thousand men, whom he had got together by liberal promises, he marched on Exeter, to which city he laid siege, in compliance with the advice of his adherents that he should endeavour to make himself master of some walled town. He sent a demand to the citizens to surrender to him, but as he had no artillery to enforce his claims, his assumed title of Richard the Fourth, King of England, inspired little reverence, and after some unsuccessful assaults he was compelled to raise the siege and hastily retire to Taunton. Seeing clearly how utterly incompetent his undisciplined forces were to compete with the veteran troops Henry was sending against him, he forsook them in the night, and, accompanied by several of his principal followers, fled to the monastery of Beaulieu, in the New Forest, and there claimed sanctuary. His followers, left without a leader, surrendered without an effort; a number of them were hanged, and the rest heavily fined.

Not daring to violate the privileges of a sanctuary,

Henry had the Beaulieu Monastery securely guarded; the meanwhile he contrived to obtain possession of the Lady Catherine Gordon, mightily afraid that she might give birth to a child, in which case, as Bacon shrewdly remarks, "the business would not have ended in Perkin's person." The politic king received the royal lady kindly, and sent her to the queen; awarded her "honourable allowance for the support of her estate, which she enjoyed both during the king's life and many years after."

Determined not to let go his hold on Perkin, the king promised him a full pardon upon condition that he confessed himself an impostor. Unable to discover any means of escape, the pretender accepted Henry's conditions, and on the 5th October surrendered to the royal troops at Taunton. He did not reach London until the end of November, and on his arrival was sent as a prisoner to the Tower. At first the supposed Richard was treated with much respect, and the evidence of his official examination kept strictly secret; although the garbled and absurd account of it which Henry caused to be published was so contradictory and generally unsatisfactory, that "men missing of that they looked for," says the chronicler, "looked about for they knew not what, and were in more doubt than before." Perkin, on his way to the Tower, was made to traverse the city on horseback, but not in any ignominious fashion; and although scoffed at by some, by the majority was treated with respect.

After about six months of detention, the pretender contrived or was permitted to escape; but such diligent pursuit was made that he was compelled to again take sanctuary, and this time in the Priory of Shene, in Surrey. As soon as his retreat was publicly known, the King was advised to take him forth and hang him, but Henry was too prudent for such a course. At the intercession of the Prior of Shene, the King promised to spare the fugitive's life, bidding them "take him forth, and set the knave in the stocks." Taken from his place of refuge, and brought back to London, the wretched youth was fettered and placed for a whole day in the stocks, and on the following day, the 14th June, 1499, was compelled to read from a scaffold, erected in Cheapside, a lengthy and rambling confession, in which, among other matters, he acknowledged himself to be Perkin, son of John Warbeck, a Flemish tradesman, and that he had been taught to enact his part by various enemies of King Henry.

After the second reading of this "confession," which was so badly composed that it served rather to confirm than dissipate the belief that the so-called "Perkin" was the personage he had assumed to be, the prisoner was again incarcerated in the Tower, where he became the companion and friend of the unfortunate Edward, Earl of Warwick, whom Lambert Simnel had formerly counterfeited. Such was the fascination of the claimant's manners that he not only won the friendship of his fellow-prisoners, but also the favour of his keepers, the four servants of Sir John Digby, the Lieutenant, who, apparently, conspired together to permit the escape of the two captives, and to aid them to excite another insurrection. The whole plot in all probability originated in the cunning of Henry, who made it a pretext for the trial and execution of both his troublesome prisoners. "The opinion of the King's great wisdom," as Bacon dexterously recounts it, " did surcharge him with a sinister fame, that Perkin was but his bait to entrap the Earl of Warwick."

About the time of this presumed plot, and most opportunely for Henry, another claimant to the name and title of the young Earl of Warwick appeared in Suffolk. Although this pretender was speedily taken and executed, the state of disquietude these events kept the country in afforded the King ample excuse for proceeding to extremities, notwithstanding the fact that the whole affair was regarded as a subtle device of the Sovereign. Accordingly, on the 16th November, 1419, Perkin was brought to trial, and was found guilty upon the indictment of having conspired, in company with the hapless Earl of Warwick, "to raise sedition and destroy the King." Upon the 23rd of the month Perkin was taken from the Tower to Tyburn, and, after having again read his confession and vouched for its truth, was executed. Such was the end of this strange drama, which was, as Bacon remarks, " one of the longest plays of that kind."

The case of Perkin Warbeck is one of the most mysterious on record; and in attempting to gauge the truth or falsity of his claim to royalty it must not be overlooked that the only contemporary records of him and his adventures are by those who professedly wrote on King Henry's behalf, and were not, therefore, likely to be over scrupulous in suppressing any facts tending to support the pretender's claims. The confession wrung from him under fear of death is of little or no value; the absence of all allusion in it to the Duchess of Burgundy seems to disprove the assertion that it was written by Perkin himself; whilst the absurd statement it contained that he, a thorough master apparently of the language, did not learn English until forced to, after his arrival at Cork, is most suspicious. He was never confronted with his supposed mother, the Queen Dowager, whom Henry had in safe keeping at Bermondsey, nor were any judicial steps taken to expose his imposture, if such it were. The King was most studiously careful to keep all records of the affair out of the people's sight; he took Tyrrell, the supposed chief murderer of the young princes, into his favour, and never had, what might have satisfied the suspicions of many, the remains of the two lads publicly exhumed. According to the account of Sir Thomas More, the murdered princes were first buried "at the stairfoot, deep in the ground, under a heap of stones," but were afterwards taken up, at the desire of King Richard, and reburied by the Tower Chaplain "privately, in a place that, by reason of his death, never came to light." This account, if true, would seem to cast a doubt upon the identity of the "small bones" discovered under the staircase in the reign of Charles the Second, and by him had interred and commemorated as the remains of the royal princes.

The circumstantial account of Lord Verulam is so enveloped in mystery and innuendo, and his desire to screen the Tudor King is so self-evident, that it has caused many, including the sophistical and shallow Walpole, to believe and assert that "Perkin Warbeck" was indeed the royal personage he claimed to be.

THE FALSE MUSTAPHA THE SECOND OF TURKEY.

A.D. 1555.

THE Sultan Soliman the First, surnamed the Legislator, raised the Turkish Empire to its highest pinnacle of glory. Owing, however, to the great extent of frontier which his dominions possessed, he was continually at war with one or the other of the neighbouring powers. In 1555 he was engaged in hostilities with Persia, but, despite his desire to pursue the contest with vigour, the weight of sixty years, and the fatigues of twelve personally conducted campaigns, rendered repose necessary to him; he, therefore, left the command of his forces to the Grand Vizier Rustem.

The repose which Soliman had promised himself did not last long; the interruption came whence it was least expected. Of his numerous sons Mustapha, his eldest, was the child of a Circassian, whilst several others were children of Roxelana, a jealous and ambitious woman. The sister of this latter woman, married to the Grand Vizier Rustem, was the link by which she succeeded in obtaining his co-operation in her schemes. Seeing every probability of Mustapha eventually obtaining the throne to the exclusion of her own sons, Roxelana determined upon his death. Conspiring with Rustem, she forged letters purporting to be addressed by the heir-apparent to a friend of his, informing him that he was treating with his father's foe, the King of Persia, with the view of obtaining one of his daughters in marriage. At the same time that this communication was adroitly placed before Soliman, he received intelligence from his Grand Vizier that Prince Mustapha displayed a disposition to revolt, and was attending complacently to the seditious propositions of the emissaries.

This startling news aroused the old hero; he immediately quitted his palace and its pleasures, placed himself once more at the head of his army, and summoned his son to his presence. On the 21st September, 1555, ignorant of the charges against him, or relying upon his innocence, the Prince arrived at his father's camp, was met by the chief captains, and conducted with all the pomp due to his rank as heir-apparent to an audience of the Sultan. On entering the imperial tent, the unfortunate man was seized by seven mutes, and strangled with a bowstring, calling vainly upon his father, who, hidden by a silken curtain, witnessed the horrible deed. Not satisfied with his son's death, the old monarch also caused his grandson Murat, Mustapha's child, to be put to death in the same way as its parent. Prince Ziangir, a younger brother of the assassinated man, was so distressed at the catastrophe, that, after reproaching his unnatural father, he committed suicide. The two princes were interred together, and a mosque erected over their remains.

The army deeply deplored the loss of the unfortunate Mustapha, who was held in great esteem, and attributing his death to the schemes of Rustem clamoured for his dismissal. Yielding to the universal indignation, Soliman consented to deprive the Grand Vizier of his post, which was bestowed on Ahmed Pacha. The general feeling of grief which the heir-apparent's death caused throughout the empire found expression in numerous poems and elegies; and amongst others Yahïa, a celebrated contemporary poet, composed verses that were known and repeated in all parts of the empire. Two years later, when Rustem returned to power, he was desirous of having Yahïa executed, but this the Sultan would not consent to; and the Grand Vizier had to satisfy his vengeance with depriving the poet of his post of Administrator of Charity to the crown.

Meanwhile the death of Mustapha, so far from having secured rest for either Soliman or the Empire, only gave rise to fresh complications. Bajazet and Selim, two sons of the infamous but clever Roxelana, both desirous of grasping the sceptre before their father's death, by means of a deep-laid conspiracy, raised the standard of revolt; and in order to obtain the sympathy and assistance of the army gave out that Mustapha, instead of being dead as was generally imagined, was alive, and heading the rebels. It was averred that the prince had been permitted to escape, someone else having been substituted in his place for execution. A man, bearing a resemblance to the deceased Mustapha, was found and taught to play the part destined for him.

The army, eager to vent its rage upon Rustem, deserted largely to the pretender, whom many officers of position recognized, or appeared to, as their veritable prince. The Sultan was equal to the emergency; he sent vigorous instructions to the governors of the provinces where the disorders were; raised large bodies of mercenaries, and, above all, sowed his gold broadcast. This latter method had the desired effect: the impostor was betrayed, and by a man whom he had created his Grand Vizier. Conducted to Constantinople, and put to the torture, the claimant revealed the whole plot. Selim fled for refuge to Persia, but was ultimately delivered up to his father for a large sum of money by the Shah; and, together with his five little sons, put to death. Bajazet's apparent contrition, and his mother Roxelana's intercession, procured his pardon; but the unfortunate instrument of his villainy, the pseudo Mustapha, was executed on the gallows.

THE FALSE SEBASTIAN OF PORTUGAL.

A.D. 1598—1603.

NO claimant's case is more remarkable than that of Don Sebastian of Portugal, exhibiting, as it does, the tenacity of tradition; for, although more than two hundred years had elapsed since their sovereign's death, hopes of his return were entertained down to the beginning of the present century by his superstitious countrymen, who cherished his memory much as the memory of those semi-mythical monarchs—Arthur of England, and Barbarossa of Germany—was cherished by their respective countrymen in the middle ages.

Don Sebastian, King of Portugal, led by an insane desire to emulate the deeds of his ancestors against the Arabs, availed himself of every opportunity of mixing in the dynastic quarrels of the Moors. In 1578, contrary to the wishes and remonstrances of his allies, relatives, and people, he accompanied an expedition to Africa, with the avowed purpose of setting the Cross above the Crescent, but virtually in hopes of gaining a warrior's renown. His first battle on the field of

Alcaçarquivir was as ill-fated as it was ill-advised; the Portuguese army was cut to pieces, and Sebastian, so it was supposed, was amongst the slain. After the fight, a corse, recognized by one of the survivors as the King's, was discovered by the victorious Moors, and forwarded by the Emperor of Morocco as a present to his ally, Philip the Second of Spain. In 1582 this monarch restored it to the Portuguese, by whom it was interred with all due solemnity in the royal mausoleum in the church of Our Lady of Belem.

The Crown of Portugal, upon the intelligence of Sebastian's death, devolved upon Don Henry, an elderly Cardinal, who, enjoying a brief reign of seventeen months, died without leaving any heirs. After a short but decisive struggle, Portugal fell an easy prey to Philip of Spain, but he was not long allowed to enjoy quiet possession of the usurped realm. The people had never credited the account of their idolized monarch's death, and rumour after rumour had been circulated to prove his existence. Three claimants to the name and title of the slain Sebastian arose, one after the other, to disturb and perplex the country, and afford the Spanish pretexts for further plunder and murder. Although these three played their part well, and occasioned the Government much trouble, there is little doubt as to their having been impostors; but over one, a fourth pretender, still hangs a cloud of impenetrable mystery.

This last aspirant appeared at Venice about twenty years after the battle of Alcaçarquivir, a very plausible account of his escape from which he was enabled to give, further stating that he had subsequently reached Portugal, and revealed his presence there to his great uncle Henry, who was then reigning; but as he had then stated that, sick and broken-hearted at his overthrow by the infidel, he had no present intention of resuming his sceptre, no notice was taken of the notification. As soon as his wounds were healed, the *soi disant* Don Sebastian stated, he, and two Portuguese nobles who were alleged to have saved themselves in his company, started on their travels, and travelled over Europe, Africa, and Asia, visiting the colonial possessions of Portugal, and even taking a personal share with the Persians in their war against the Turks. The King also paid visits to the Grand Llama of Thibet, and to Prester John in Ethiopia, encountering no end of marvellous adventures on his journeys, during which, however, his two companions, worn out with wounds and fatigues, succumbed to death. The royal wanderer then retired to a hermitage in the Georgian desert, and stayed there until the year 1597, when, admonished by a dream to resume his crown, he returned to Europe. He landed in Sicily, and at once despatched letters to several of his most attached nobles in Portugal. Catizoni, his messenger, was arrested on landing, and never heard of again; but through some unknown channels the tidings of which he was the bearer transpired, and threw the whole country into a profound state of excitement. Had the *soi disant* monarch had courage to have landed in Portugal at this time, it is pretty generally believed that, whatever may have been the value of his claims to the name of Don Sebastian, the whole people would have acknowledged his rights; as one writer says, the nation "would have acknowledged a negro to be their lost king, so that he delivered them from the hated rule of the Spaniards."

Wanting the resolution, or the means, to seek Portugal, the claimant fell from one state of wretchedness to another, until, at last, it is averred he was discovered by some compatriots in Padua selling pies in the street for a livelihood. Convinced that they had discovered their legitimate sovereign, the Portuguese residents and exiles at once acknowledged his claims, and supplied him with all the necessaries of life. Apprised of this event, the Spanish ambassador immediately requested the Venetian senate to banish the "insolent adventurer" from their states. The Podesta of Padua being commanded by the

Seignory to banish from his city within three days "a man calling himself falsely Sebastian, King of Portugal," and this mandate being communicated to the *soi disant* monarch, he boldly repaired to Venice, and requested the Senate, the only free tribunal in Europe, to investigate his claims. Upon his arrival, he was seized and thrown into a dungeon, at the instance of Philip's ambassador, who suborned witnesses to accuse him of horrible crimes. This, however, caused his pretensions to be speedily noised about all over Europe. A large number of the Portuguese in Italy presented several petitions to the Senate, calling upon it to investigate the prisoner's claims, whilst Sampayo, a Dominican of considerable influence in Padua, wrote and published a full statement of the facts, and dedicated it to the potentates of Europe.

In the meantime the Spaniards were not idle. They averred that the claimant was a Calabrese impostor, of bad repute, if not a renegade monk; they alluded to the gross improbabilities in his story, and the little likelihood there was of Sebastian, even if he had escaped from the battle of Alcacarquivir, remaining out of the pale of civilization for twenty years without affording anyone an intimation of his existence. They pointed out that the pretender's Portuguese was anything but pure, and that whereas

Sebastian's complexion was fair this man's was dark.

Sampayo, on behalf of the prisoner, replied that the king's wounded pride at his defeat, and youthful feelings of self-dependence, had carried him into all his romantic wanderings, whilst his fair complexion and native accent had necessarily changed during twenty years' rambling in the sultry lands which he had visited.

Whilst this discussion was going on, the prisoner was being severely examined by the Venetian Senate, and displayed, so all averred, such knowledge of their most secret dealings with the true Don Sebastian as fairly startled them. He declared himself ready to undergo the punishment of death if his claims were proved to be unfounded, and petitioned that he might be personally examined for any marks which the King of Portugal had been known to possess. The Portuguese residents warmly supporting the latter part of the memorial, the Seignory granted their request, and sent Sampayo with a safe conduct to Lisbon to ascertain these distinctive marks, and to get a written declaration of them signed by competent people. After an absence of two months the Dominican returned, with an attestation, witnessed by persons who had been attached to the late royal household, and countersigned by the apostolical notary, as a proof of the document's genuineness.

During Sampayo's absence the Spanish Government had made such forcible representations to the Venetian Senate, that on his return the Doge stated "it did not beseem the Republic to take cognizance of the claims of the pretender to the Portuguese Crown, unless at the request of a member of the family of European potentates." Nothing daunted, the unwearied envoy of the *soi disant* Sebastian undertook a journey to Holland to procure the intervention of the House of Nassau. His exertions were aided by the warm support of several Portuguese nobles, and by the influence of Henry the Fourth of France, who, through his ambassador at Venice, intimated that if the Dutch intercession failed, France would take the claimant under her protection. The States of Holland, however, having requested the Italian Republic to proceed with the inquiry, the Spanish ambassador withdrew his protest, and commissioners were appointed to examine the prisoner for the bodily peculiarities which the king was known to have possessed.

These peculiarities were alleged to be "a right hand longer and larger than the left; the upper part of the arms longer than the part between the elbow and the wrist; a deep scar above the right eyebrow;

a tooth missing from the lower jaw, and a large excrescence or wart on the instep of the right foot." An investigation of the prisoner was then made, in the presence of Sampayo, by four Venetian officers of justice; and they reported that not only were all these peculiarities found upon him, but that his head and face bore the scars of sabre wounds; whilst, when his jaw was being examined, he had asked whether Sebastian Nero, the Court barber at Lisbon, who had extracted the tooth, was still alive.

The next day this evidence was laid before the senate, which held a secret deliberation of four days' duration, shared in by the Spanish ambassador and Don Christavaõ de Portugal, an apparent advocate of the captive. The threats of Philip are alleged to have overpowered the intentions of the Seignory, and, accordingly when, at ten o'clock at night, on the fourth day of the conference, the claimant was brought before them, they, without expressing any opinion respecting his identity with Don Sebastian, simply repeated the mandate formerly sent to the Podesta of Padua, banishing the person who styled himself King of Portugal from the Venetian states within the space of three days. Sampayo, and the Portuguese with him, declare that a seat was provided for the prisoner; and that whilst he remained covered during the reading of the decree the senators stood around respectfully. This averred deference, and the evasion of a direct award after so lengthy and solemn an assemblage, confirmed even waverers in the belief that the pretender was indeed the true Sebastian.

Whatever may have been the belief or reason of the senate, they contented themselves with banishing the *soi disant* monarch, and refused to deliver him up to the Spanish ambassador. Countenanced by all the enemies of Spain, the claimant now sought refuge in Tuscany, *en route*, it is said, to Rome, to claim the protection and recognition of his claims by the reigning Pontiff, Clement the Eighth. The Grand Duke Ferdinand, desirous of propitiating his powerful foe Philip, is alleged to have made an agreement with him, that if the adventurer entered the Tuscan territories he should be at once arrested and delivered up to the custody of the Spanish. Be this as it may, the pretender was seized as he was attempting to leave the Grand Duke's dominions, put on board a small frigate, taken to Naples, and delivered up to the Conde de Lemos, Philip's viceroy.

The unfortunate man, according to popular story, was placed in a dungeon, and starved for three days, in order to compel him to confess his imposture. When the three days had expired he was visited by the Auditor-General, and urged to acknowledge his fraud. "Do with me as you please, and say what you will, I am King Sebastian," is reported to have been his response. Subsequently taken before the Viceroy, he is alleged to have referred to certain secret political transactions which took place at Lisbon when the Conde de Lemos had been ambassador there. Notwithstanding this revelation, the Conde affirmed his conviction that "the prisoner was an impostor;" but had him transferred from his dungeon to a pleasant chamber overlooking the Bay of Naples, and allotted him the sum of five crowns daily for his support.

For a twelvemonth the claimant was left in peaceful possession of his cell, when another insurrection breaking out in the Portuguese possessions, a mandate arrived from Madrid, directing the claimant to be returned to his dungeon, and again interrogated. He persisted in his protestations, and begged to be sent to Lisbon, where his statements might be strictly investigated. This was refused, and sentence pronounced upon him as "a vagabond, impostor, and liar;" and he was condemned to the galleys for life, after being paraded through the streets of Naples on an ass, whilst his imposture was proclaimed by the public crier. On the 17th April, 1602, this punishment was carried out. "Behold the justice and severity of his Catholic Majesty! He commands that this miserable man shall be degraded and condemned for life to the galleys, because he falsely and flagitiously declares himself to be the late Don Sebastian, King of Portugal, when he is but a vile impostor from Calabria!" was the proclamation made as the prisoner was taken through the streets of Naples. He was then clothed in the garb of a galley slave, and, according to some authorities, publicly flogged, all the while calmly and positively reiterating his assertion that he was Sebastian, King of Portugal.

According to contemporary chronicles, his head was then shaved, and his hands and feet put in irons; he was then sent to the galleys, and compelled to row. He was afterwards carried on board a vessel and taken to St. Lucar, at that time the largest convict station of Spain. During the voyage the prisoner's irons were removed, and his labours suspended. When the galley arrived at St. Lucar, the Duke and Duchess of Medina Sidonia are asserted to have seen the captive and conversed with him; and a curious story is told of the interview. The Duke and his consort had formerly given Don Sebastian a magnificent entertainment when on his ill-fated expedition to Africa, and the Portuguese monarch had then presented a sword to his host and a valuable ring to the Duchess.

Upon the claimant's arrival at St. Lucar, the Duke desired to be allowed to try and select him from amongst the other felons, but failed to recognize him. The *soi disant* King was then introduced to the nobleman and his wife, and recounted many incidents of their interview with Don Sebastian. He asked the Duke if he still possessed the sword which he had presented him upon that occasion, saying that he could identify it if conducted to the ducal armoury. Hearing this the Duke called for several swords, but upon their production the prisoner exclaimed, " My sword is not amongst these!" Another quantity of swords, this time including the veritable weapon, were now produced, and, so runs the story, the weapon was instantly recognized and unsheathed by the claimant. He then reminded the Duchess of the ring given her by Sebastian as a memento of his visit, and asked if she still retained it. She thereupon sent for her jewel-case and desired him to select it from amongst more than a hundred rings which it contained, and this he did immediately.

The Duke and Duchess of Medina Sidonia, it is averred, then departed sadly, and sorrowing at such an evidently unjust detention; but it is somewhat singular, and throws much doubt upon the anecdote, that no record appears of them having ever attempted to obtain an amelioration of the captive's lot, which, from their position and interest at the Spanish court, they could, undoubtedly, have procured.

The unfortunate pretender was now removed to Seville, but Sampayo having excited an insurrection in Portugal, he was again taken to St. Lucar, and on the 20th April, 1603, was hanged from its highest bastion. The Dominican, and several other of the claimant's adherents, suffered the same fate shortly afterwards.

THE FALSE DEMETRIUS OF RUSSIA.

A.D. 1603—1606.

IVAN THE TERRIBLE of Russia, having murdered his eldest son, left the crown to the next, Feodore, a prince so feeble in body and mind that the government of the country had to be committed to the care of his brother-in-law, Boris. This bold and unscrupulous man aspired to the throne, but between him and the imbecile who occupied it stood Demetrius, another child of the late monarch. The Regent left this boy to the care of his mother, the Dowager Czarina, under whose charge he attained to the age of ten. One afternoon of May 1591, the child was playing with four other boys in the palace courtyard, his governess, nurse, and another female servant being close by. According to the testimony of these persons he had a knife in his hand. For a moment he disappeared, and the next instant was discovered dying, with a large wound in his throat; he died without uttering a word. Suspicion of foul play was at once aroused, and some known emissaries of Boris being discovered in the neighbourhood, they fell victims to the fury of the populace. The Regent instituted an inquiry, and the result was a verdict that the boy had died from a wound accidentally inflicted upon himself. The towns-people were either put to death or dispersed for their hasty judgment upon the supposed assassins, the palace was razed to the ground, the flourishing town turned into a desert, and the Dowager Czarina forced into a convent. The slovenly way in which the inquiry had been made, the fact that it had been conducted by creatures of Boris, that the body was never examined, nor the knife compared with the wound, together with the attempted obliteration of all surrounding dwellings, afford very strong evidence that a murder had been done, and by the instigation of the Regent; but that Demetrius died there can scarcely be the shadow of a doubt.

After seven years Feodore died, and Boris succeeded in obtaining the vacant throne. Hated and feared by all classes, the whole country was longing for a change from his tyrannical rule, when a rumour came from the Lithuanian frontier that Demetrius, believed to have been murdered at Uglitch, was still alive, and in Poland. Amid the many contradictory reports, one main fact was positively proclaimed—that was, the young prince was alive, and preparing to contend for the throne of his ancestors.

The story which this aspirant to empire gave to Prince Adam Wiszniswiecki, of Brahin, in Lithuania, in whose employ he was, was that the physician in attendance upon him (Demetrius), having been solicited by Boris to destroy him, consented, but instead of doing so, substituted the body of a serf's child for that of the to-be-slain prince, and safely carried off the heir presumptive, and placed him in the charge of a faithful adherent of the royal family. Unfortunately, both the physician and the faithful guardian being dead, the tale had to be received for what it was worth; nevertheless, the unknown produced a Russian seal, bearing the name and arms of the Czarevitch, and a valuable jewelled cross. This was in the summer of 1603, when Demetrius, if living, would have been about twenty-two—an age apparently corresponding with that of the claimant to his name. Visitors arrived who quickly recognized their resuscitated prince; warts which the late Emperor's son had had on the forehead, and under the right eye, were discovered, whilst one arm being longer than another was a still surer sign. The deportment and acquirements of the young pretender were suited to his birth, not the least of them being his good horsemanship and skill in fencing. The Poles, ready for mischief, espoused his cause; George, the

Palatine of Sandomir, gave him his daughter in marriage, and the Pope of Rome, upon his secret confession of the Catholic faith, sanctioned his pretensions. Thus encouraged, he invaded Russia with a small force, and, assisted by a variety of conflicting circumstances, including the sudden death of Boris, in the course of a few months found himself the undisputed master of the whole empire. On the 20th of June, 1605, the adventurer entered Moscow in state, amid the acclamations of believing multitudes. On entering the church of St. Michael, the pseudo Demetrius, according to all accounts, acted his part admirably; kneeling before the tomb of Ivan, his face suffused with tears, he clasped his hands and exclaimed, "O father! thy orphan reigns!—this he owes to thy holy prayers!" The audience was convinced, sobbed in unison, and from all sides arose the cry, "He is the son of the Terrible!"

But a still more formidable test was to be undergone. The Dowager Czarina forsook the convent in which she had so long been immured to behold the man claiming to be her son. Demetrius went to meet her in regal state, and their first interview took place in a magnificent tent, specially prepared for the interesting ceremony. After they had been left together for a few minutes they came out, and threw themselves into one another's arms, in the full view of the enormous multitude which had assembled. Ivan's widow had recognized her son, and the new monarch was master of the situation. He respectfully conducted the Czarina to a carriage, walking bareheaded by its side. In the capital he treated her with every attention, visited her daily, and provided her with a competent revenue to maintain her royal dignity. A few moments after the murder of her son at Uglitch, she was on the spot and recognized the body; and yet, after having maintained for fourteen years her belief in his death, she came forward and recognized him in the successful adventurer, at the exact instant that recantation was worth any price.

Demetrius now set to work to govern with humanity and justice; both qualities quite unsuited to Russian tastes, who soon grew as tired of their new Czar as they had been of his predecessors. He appears to have been an able and forbearing man, but he outraged the nobles by pointing out their educational deficiencies, and the Greek priesthood by a careless or irreverent demeanour towards their Church. This latter error was his ruin. The treasury being exhausted, he began to cast wistful glances at the swollen revenues of the clergy, who at once determined upon his destruction.

On the 29th of May, 1606, "Death to the heretic!" rang through the streets of Moscow. The excited mobs, headed by priests and Shuiski, a discontented noble, who had previously been pardoned for conspiracy, broke into the palace, hunted their prey from room to room, until, already bleeding from a sabre wound, the unfortunate victim leaped out of a window into the court below, a height of thirty feet. He broke his leg in the fall, and fainted. The insurgents speedily found him, dragged him mid curses and blows into the palace, dressed him in a pastrycook's caftan in mockery, and taunted him as to his birth. The wretched man, collecting his strength, exclaimed, "I am your Czar, the son of Ivan Vassilievitch!" when his agony was terminated by a shot from an arquebuss.

His followers were destroyed, his wife barely escaped with life, and every kind of indignity was offered to the Polish ladies in attendance upon her. The body of the murdered man, after lying exposed for some days, was unceremoniously buried without the walls, then disinterred and burnt, the ashes collected, and, to make sure of no further resuscitation, mixed with gunpowder and fired off from a cannon.

Shuiski, the leader of the revolution, was raised to the throne, but finding the memory of his predecessor still cherished by many, he sought to eradicate the feeling by proving him an impostor. The Dowager Czarina, ever complacent, gave him a written declaration that the deposed Czar was not her son; but the nation placed little reliance upon her testimony now. Shuiski then pretended to have discovered the body of young Demetrius in the ruins of Uglitch, and his clerical friends contrived a miracle for the occasion. When the body was brought to Moscow, they recognized the corpse as that of the real prince, and affirmed that by heavenly providence it had been preserved in its then condition—it being found quite uncorrupt, and the glow of life not even faded from the cheek. But this miraculous interposition did not satisfy everybody, and whilst the partizans of the late Czar were affirming that a body had been substituted for the occasion, the whole country was roused to a state of frenzy by a rumour that the conspirators had murdered, burnt, and fired from the cannon's mouth *the wrong man!*

This time a substituted corpse could not be produced. A civil war broke out, but it was some time before a suitable claimant could be discovered. At last a Lithuanian Jew was selected by the insurgents, who, aided by the Poles, advanced into Russia at the head of a large army. A feasible story was invented to account for the escape of the intended victim of the late massacre; and to confirm the nation in the belief of his identity with their late Czar, Marina, the widowed Czarina, publicly acknowledged him as her own Demetrius, lived with him as his consort, and had a child by him. Her father, the Palatine of Sandomir, also recognized him as his son-in-law, and in a short time almost the whole empire declared for him.

His reign, however, was short. Deserted by his foreign allies, he was forced to fly, and eventually was assassinated. His consort, Marina, died in prison, and Ivan, one of their children, although only three years old, was publicly hanged—the most ghastly act in the entire tragedy!

DEMETRIUS THE YOUNGER OF RUSSIA.

A.D. 1632—1653.

THE account of this unfortunate young man is as romantic as any novelist could possibly desire. Its full details are probably only to be found in one work, and that one a work of great rarity and antiquity, by Jean Baptiste de Rocoles, historiographer of France in the latter part of the seventeenth century. The recital of Monsieur de Rocoles acquires greater interest from the fact that he himself derived a portion of his particulars from eye-witnesses, including the account of the hero's death, which was witnessed by an Austrian colonel named Bertrand.

According to the most reliable accounts of the defeat and overthrow of the second false Demetrius, his wife Marina was cast into prison, and their infant son, only three years old, publicly hanged. If this were true, and the following history veracious, the Czarina must have given birth to a second son whilst in captivity; but there does not appear to be any historic evidence on the point. The pretender always styled himself the son of the Czar Demetrius;

not, of course, in any way admitting that there were two pseudo Demetriuses.

"The time of the confusion," as it is styled in Russian history, was fruitful in the production of such impostors. Besides the two more important claimants already spoken of, and the man whose story claims this chapter, another false Demetrius was started, under Polish protection, in 1611; and a short time before that, a claimant to the title of Czarevitch Peter appeared, and alleged that he was a son of the Czar Feodor the First; but after some short-lived success both perished.

According to the account of De Rocoles, the Czarina Marina, when thrown into prison by the murderers of her husband, escaped maltreatment by alleging that she was *enceinte*. This excuse was sufficient to preserve her from the terrible fate which befel many of her female attendants, but she was carefully guarded henceforth by her captors, who only waited for her child's birth to immediately put an end to its existence. Well aware of the fate which awaited her unborn babe, the ex-Czarina procured the body of a dead infant, and at her *accouchement* had it substituted for the male child which she gave birth to.

The newly-born boy was confided to the care of a Cossack woman, the mother of the dead babe, and was duly baptized Demetrius by a priestly confidant, and indelibly marked on the shoulder with a cross, to enable its royal birth to be proved when the opportunity arose. Some little time after this Marina found herself dying, and on her deathbed she confided to her attendants the stratagem by which she had preserved her son's life, and by them the secret was re-told to the Poles, who, four or five years later, came to Moscow with General Stanislas Solskonski. In the meanwhile, the Cossack to whom young Demetrius had been confided, and who brought him up in ignorance of his paternity, died without having any opportunity, or at all events availing herself of it, to reveal the secret of the boy's birth.

The year 1632 arrived, and the youthful Demetrius had nearly attained his twenty-sixth year. Going one day, by chance, to bathe in a small river in the vicinity of the little town of Samburg, in Black Russia, where he lived, another bather drew attention to the marks on his shoulder, and upbraided him for coming to bathe with honest men, deeming that he had been branded for some crime. The poor young man endeavoured to excuse himself by protesting that he had been born with this cross on his shoulder, as, indeed, he believed he had; and upon his companions examining the marks, they perceived that, though they were legible, they were quite different to anything they had ever seen upon the body of a malefactor. The story of the strange cross upon the young man's shoulder was soon noised about all over the neighbourhood, and coming to the ears of John Danielonski, the Royal Treasurer, he desired to see Demetrius. A number of his domestics were sent after the unknown, and he was soon found and taken before the grand official, where the poverty of his attire, and the wretchedness of his condition, were apparent to all.

The Treasurer, having some presentiment or knowledge of the way in which the young Demetrius had been marked, spoke to the young man kindly, and bidding him cast off all fear, asked to be allowed to see the said figuring upon his shoulder. The unknown, who was of handsome form and features, drew open his poor vest, and baring his shoulder, showed the marks which had been tattooed upon him at birth. Danielonski was enabled to trace the cross, but could not decipher the letters of which it was formed. A Russian priest, however, being found, he quickly read them, and affirmed that they stood for "Demetrius, son of the Czar Demetrius."

The joy of the Treasurer was immense at having discovered a son of the late Czar; he kissed the hands of the astounded prince, wished him every happiness, and placed all that could be wished for at his disposal. The joyous tidings spread in every direction; a courier was at once despatched to Vladislas the Fourth, who was then King of Poland, and the young man's claims bruited about everywhere. Vladislas, only too glad of an opportunity to annoy Alexis, the then Czar of Moscovy, sent at once for the young claimant to come to his court at Warsaw, and on his arrival awarded him an equipage suited to his presumed dignity. When the pseudo Czarewitch appeared at court, decked out in all his newly-acquired finery, he excited favourable attention by his handsome looks and kindly behaviour. He contracted a firm friendship with the nephew of the Grand Khan of Tartary, who, having been ousted from his possessions by an uncle, had sought and found an asylum in the Polish court. An apparent similarity of misfortune drew them together, and Vladislas, doubtlessly finding it suit his policy to encourage their pretensions, treated the two young men with every kindness, protested that he regarded them as sons, he not having any of his own, and declared that he would not leave anything undone to replace them upon their respective thrones.

Intelligence of the arrival and friendly reception of Demetrius at the Polish court was not long in travelling to Moscow; the Czar was greatly enraged when he heard of what had occurred, and sent an envoy to Vladislas to demand that the person of the *soi disant* Czarewitch should be given up to him. The Latin address which the Moscovite ambassador delivered to the Polish King when he made his demand is still preserved, and is chiefly remarkable for the hundred and one titles by which the Russian monarch was designated. Vladislas responded to the wearisome harangue in the same language, to the effect that no consideration would induce him to hand Prince Demetrius over to his rival Alexis, and he took no pains to conceal from the envoy that he meant to support the claims of his guest as far as lay in his power. The fruitlessness of this mission gave great uneasiness to the Czar, and caused him to seek out every possible alliance. Fate soon assisted him.

In 1648 Vladislas died, and was succeeded on the Polish throne by John Casimir, who, having to fight with Charles of Sweden, and other European powers, found it necessary to secure the neutrality of Russia; he was, therefore, obliged to banish Demetrius. The unfortunate man at first took refuge in Revel, in the little republic of Livonia. The magistrates and principal citizens received him with regal honours, but, on their refusal to deliver him up to the Czar, were threatened by that potentate with war. Reluctantly his hosts were compelled to request their luckless guest to seek another asylum, but on his departure they made him handsome presents, and had him safely and honourably escorted to the seaport of Riga.

The innocent impostor, as he has been termed, now made his way to Sweden, but political reasons drove him quickly thence, and he next sought safety with the Duke of Holstein Gottorp. He met with a friendly reception, but the fates had timed his visit at a most inopportune moment. The Duke had recently negotiated a treaty of commerce with the Czar, and while engaged on the embassy, Eurchmann, one of his envoys, had pledged his master's credit, without his authority, for a large sum of money, variously stated at one hundred thousand and three hundred thousand crowns; for which misdeed, upon his return to Holstein, he was decapitated. The Duke was, or appeared to be, in a state of embarrassment as to the liquidation of the debt, when a Russian agent, who was residing at Lubeck, and knew the value of the claimant to the Russian Czar, opened negotiations with Holstein's ruler, and, pretending to the only too willing prince that his guest was merely a common impostor, arranged for his delivery to

Alexis in exchange for the receipts of the money brought away and owed for by his envoy. This is the common account of the nefarious transaction, but in all probability the whole affair had been previously arranged between the two sovereigns, and Eurchmann and Demetrius were the victims of the royal plot.

Be the truth what it may, suffices to say that the Duke of Holstein seized Demetrius, and delivered him up to the Russians sent to receive him, obtaining in return the bills for the money owing. The unfortunate man was hurried on board a vessel, transported to the Russian coast, and taken thence by rapid stages to Moscow. Directly he arrived in the metropolis the captive had a wooden gag forced into his mouth to prevent him speaking, and was confronted by an old woman, bribed for the purpose, who declared herself to be his mother, and upbraided him for unnatural ingratitude to her, and his presumption in disowning his parent; finally, desiring him to avow his misdeeds, and not to let her endure the misery of beholding him executed for his imposture.

Averting his head, Demetrius showed plainly by significant gestures that he neither acknowledged her claims, nor heeded them; whilst to the priests, who addressed him in a similar strain, and urged him to confess his imposture, he simply responded by uplifting his eyes and hands towards heaven, as if resigning himself to its decree. The unhappy man was then taken out on to the great esplanade in front of the castle of Moscow, and there executed on the 31st of December, 1653, in the forty-seventh year of his age.

The Czar Alexis was not contented with the mere death of his hapless rival, but had his head severed from his body, which was quartered and elevated upon four poles, whilst portions of his remains were left scattered on the frozen ground as a repast for the dogs. The Polish ambassador, who that same day had audience of the vindictive Emperor, was conducted to the place of execution, and shown all that now remained of the unfortunate being whom his late master had so delighted to honour.

The biographer of this pseudo Demetrius finds no little pleasure in recording that the Russian agent who negotiated the sale of our hero met with a miserable death, " in punishment for causing innocent blood to be shed;" that John Casimir, the King of Poland, who first drove him from his place of safety, was obliged to abdicate his throne, and that the Duke of Holstein was despoiled of his domains by his brother-in-law, Christian the Fifth of Denmark. He moreover records the general opinion that unless the execution of Demetrius had taken place as quickly as it did—that had it only been delayed for two hours—the populace would have risen against Alexis to despoil him of his kingdom, and place his victim on the throne in his stead.

It is a somewhat more agreeable pendant to this wretched story to know that the old companion in misfortune of Demetrius, the nephew of the Grand Khan of Tartary, ultimately succeeded to the throne of his uncle, and that he seized every occasion of expressing his hatred of John Casimir for having abandoned the beloved *protégé* of his brother Vladislas.

THE FALSE ZAGA CHRIST, OF ABYSSINIA.

A.D. 1635.

THE extremely romantic and improbable story of this *soi disant* prince is derived from the highly interesting work of De Rocoles; but unsupported, as would appear to be the case, by any evidence beyond the verbal testimony of the claimant himself, it may be safely regarded as purely fictitious. Nevertheless, the fact that his pretensions to royalty were, to some extent, recognized in various parts of Europe, entitles him to a place here.

According to De Rocoles, and the monks who favoured the pretender's story, his father Jacob had reigned peaceably over Abyssinia for seven years, when, having allowed it to transpire that he proposed extirpating the Roman Catholics, Susneos, a cousin of his, who had leagued himself with that body, availed himself of the pretext to commence a civil war; and the result of it, in 1608, was the defeat and death of Jacob, and the usurpation of the crown by the victor. The deceased monarch left two sons—Cosme, aged eighteen; and Zaga Christ, or *The Treasure of Christ*, aged sixteen.

At the time of their father's death the two princes were at Aich, in the Isle of Merse, where they resided for educational purposes. The new Emperor, beginning his reign by putting several of his predecessor's adherents to death, caused Jacob's widow to fear for the safety of her sons; she therefore sent trusty messengers to them with a quantity of gold and precious stones, and bid them quit the country for a more secure asylum until their friends had rallied sufficiently to recover them their patrimony. Acting on this advice, the two princes forsook Aich; Cosme going in a southerly direction, by which route, it is asserted, he ultimately reached the Cape of Good Hope; and Zaga Christ going northwards.

Traversing the kingdom of Senaar, which was alleged to have been tributary to his father, Zaga continued his journey to Tungi, where Orbat, a pagan monarch, reigned. This king, who also was a vassal of the Abyssinian ruler, received the fugitive prince with great honours, and for some months entertained him magnificently, having conceived the design of giving him his daughter in marriage, and assisting him to regain his father's dominions. The claimant, according to his own account, declined the proffered honour because the princess was an idolater. This rare example of royal abstinence naturally enraged Orbat, who threw his guest into prison, and sent to inform the usurper that Zaga was a captive in his hands.

As soon as he received this intelligence, Susneos sent a company of guards to Orbat's capital to take possession of his young relative. Zaga, however, being warned by a friendly Venetian, who was serving under the usurper, managed, or was permitted, to elude his captors, and, accompanied by a large body of followers, after a series of dangerous adventures contrived to reach a portion of the Turkish domain. Desirous of traversing Arabia Deserta, with a view of reaching Egypt, the young wanderer now dismissed all his followers with the exception of fifty, who elected to share his dangers. A few days after this little band had penetrated into the desert, the greater portion of its baggage was stolen by a native chieftain; and some days later, in seeking for water, fifteen out of the fifty men were lost through the giving way of the cistern walls. After a tedious and trying passage, however, the devoted band succeeded in reaching a small town on the Egyptian frontiers.

After a rest of three months, the young pretender pursued his journey to Cairo, where a large body of his countrymen and co-religionists resided. Zaga was enthusiastically received by his compatriots, whilst the Turkish pacha, or governor of the city, treated him with every respect, and for several days even lodged him in his own palace. After a short stay at Cairo, the young prince started for Jerusalem, taking with him only fifteen servitors, the remainder electing to stay with their brethren in Egypt. A large number of pilgrims also accompanied the caravan, which reached the Holy City safely about Lent, 1632.

The *soi disant* prince, followed by all his adherents, took up his abode with the Abyssinian priests then resident in Jerusalem. His servants, who appeared to treat him with immense deference, are described at this stage of his adventures. They are represented as great black men, attired in blue cotton shirts, wound round with yellow *bouracan*, six or eight yards long by one wide, and with turbans of check silk. Attended by these men, Zaga called on the pacha of Jerusalem to pay his respects, and in the same style honoured with his presence, during Holy Week, the ceremonies performed at the Holy Sepulchre by the Christians. After having spent some time in Jerusalem, he began to imbibe conscientious scruples as to the Abyssinian forms of Christianity, and at last requested the chief Roman Catholic priest in the city to receive him into the communion of that Church. This, however, was refused, the Catholics fearing that the pacha might take umbrage at so important a conversion, and make use of it to instigate a persecution against them. Nevertheless, desirous of not losing so exalted a convert, the priests persuaded Zaga Christ to quit the Holy City secretly, and, accompanied by some other pilgrims and the two or three servants who still followed his fortunes, to repair to Nazareth, where he would have perfect liberty to make his profession, the place being under the domination of Emir Fechraddin, an independent chief.

On the second Thursday after Easter, 1632, the *soi disant* prince arrived in Nazareth, and resided there until September of the same year; during which time he learnt to read, write, and speak a little French and Italian. It is stated that after Zaga had spent a few days at the Convent of Nazareth, the said religious house was visited by an Armenian bishop and his train, who were returning from solemnizing Easter at Jerusalem. The prince, meeting the ecclesiastic in the church, reproached him bitterly for teaching his countrymen such manifold lies and errors, such as that the sacred fire at the Holy City was sent from heaven instead of being merely ignited with a common flint, and so forth. The priest left Zaga without being able to make any reply; but in revenge for the affront he had received, he went to the prince's few remaining followers, informed them that their master had determined to pass into Europe and become a Roman Catholic, and warned them against accompanying the heretic; as Europe was, he told them, a country of perpetual frost and snow, where natives of warmer climes would speedily die, even if they escaped being captured by the corsairs, and sold as galley-slaves, whilst on the journey. Moreover, he threatened them with excommunication if they continued to associate with such a renegade to the true and pure faith.

Thus frightened, the poor Abyssinians went to their master, and represented to him that they should have to quit him if he determined to leave for Europe, as they neither wished to be frozen to death nor made galley-slaves of. Their master wept at this discourse, and reproached them for their idea of abandoning him after having so long shared his fortunes; they, the only three left out of all those who had left Abyssinia with him. He pointed out to them that if they went with him they would only have the same risks he would have himself of dying through cold, or of being sold into slavery; and that it would be far better for them to live amongst fellow-Christians than with Mohammedans, who might any day massacre them all. They were much afflicted at their master's grief, but the persuasions of the cunning Armenian were too much for them; they abandoned their master to his fate, and followed the priest to Aleppo, where two of them died, and the third returned to Jerusalem.

Thus left alone, Zaga took up his abode in the convent, where he finally abjured the heresies of the Abyssinian Church, and, on St. Peter's Day, 1632, received communion and absolution in the Catholic faith. During the five months that the prince was residing at Nazareth he was the subject of ceaseless plots and schemes, in which the Abyssinians at Jerusalem took the chief part. They tried, under various pretexts, to persuade the pacha of that city to obtain possession of Zaga; but as the convent was under the protection of a friendly chief, the Emir Fechraddin, he would not undertake or permit the expedition; and at last the prince, in obedience to an invitation from the Pope, crossed over to Italy, and was received at Rome with great magnificence, the head of the Church placing a palace at his disposal.

For two years the supposed prince was hospitably entertained in the Eternal City, and at the end of that time he accepted the invitation of the Duke de Cregui, the French ambassador, to visit France. Zaga made the journey, and for three more years resided in Paris, caressed and supported by the French. Going to Ruël, a village near the capital, to pay his court to Cardinal Richelieu, he was attacked by pleurisy, and died there in 1638, at the age of about twenty-eight years. He had been supported royally during his residence in France, and now, at his death, was interred by the side of a prince of Portugal, and a monument erected over his remains. The epitaph, however, placed upon the tomb of our *soi disant* prince, expressed public opinion faithfully by doubting the justness of his claims to royal lineage.

THE FALSE IBRAHIM OF TURKEY.

A.D. 1644.

THE story of this pseudo prince is no less romantic than those of the other claimants mentioned in this work, but it differs from most of them inasmuch as the hero of it was an innocent victim rather than a conscious impostor. His history has been variously stated, some works asserting that the man was the eldest son of the Sultan Ibrahim of Turkey, and elder brother of Mehemet the Fourth, whilst others, including De Rocoles (the chief authority for our version) describe him as the illegitimate child of some unknown personage.

Tumbel Aga, according to the account given by De Rocoles, was chief of the eunuchs to the Sultan Ibrahim, as he had also been to his predecessor, Sultan Amurath. Having had occasionally to employ a certain well-known merchant of Constantinople, named Cesi, to execute various commissions for the imperial seraglio, he fancied he might entrust him with a delicate matter on his own behalf, and accordingly favoured him with instructions to procure him as pretty and modest a maiden as he could purchase in the market, regardless of cost. It is, of course, difficult to say what the Aga's object was in giving so strange a commission to Cesi, nor is it material to the story to know whether the girl was to be presented to the Sultan as a gift, or whether she was to be retained as an ornament for Tumbel's own abode. The merchant speedily informed the would-be purchaser that he had obtained a girl— a Russian, named Sciabas—who was as modest as she was beautiful. Delighted at this intelligence, the Aga paid the price demanded, and had his purchase sent to his rooms. Her beauty and manners were everything that could be desired, but Tumbel had not long had his purchase home before he discovered that she was likely to increase his household in a way neither wished for nor calculated upon. Indignant at the deception which had been practised upon him, but probably somewhat softened by the beautiful captive's manner, the old Aga pretended to chase her out of the seraglio, but meanwhile gave private orders that she should be cared for in every respect.

About five or six months after the *accouchement* of Sciabas, her master paid her a visit, and was so charmed with the beauty of her child, a handsome boy—or, what is more probable, fancied he should be enabled to recoup himself for his expenditure by the sale of both mother and infant—that he ordered every care to be taken of them. All his efforts to discover the paternity of the boy were useless; Sciabas would not gratify his curiosity, and nobody else, apparently, could.

About this time the Sultana presented her husband with a boy, for whom the Aga was instructed to procure a nurse. He recommended Sciabas, doubtless to repay himself for his outlay, and, accordingly, the young Russian and her baby took up their abode in the imperial apartments, where, indeed, they continued to live for about two years. The child of Sciabas inherited not only her beauty, but also her gentle temper; in which he contrasted so favourably with young Mehemet, the Grand Sultana's child, that the Sultan noticed the difference, and began to display a preference for it over his own offspring. The wife speedily discovered this alienation of the Sultan's affection, and not only vented her rage on the innocent objects of it, whom she ejected from the imperial apartments, but determined to avenge herself, on the first convenient opportunity, upon the Aga for having introduced them. Tumbel was not slow in perceiving his danger, and in order to escape it, requested the

Sultan to allow him to make a pilgrimage to Mecca, doubtless not intending to return to Constantinople. Ibrahim was loath to let him go, as he greatly valued his services, and, according to the custom of the Ottoman court, the slave who is permitted by the Sultan to make this sacred journey becomes a free man, and is assigned an annual pension. Nothing daunted by refusal, Tumbel renewed his request, offering to go as a captive, promising that on his return he would resume his duties at the seraglio. Ultimately the Sultan gave his consent, and the Aga made grand preparations for his journey.

When everything was ready, Tumbel embarked on board a vessel bound for Alexandria, taking with him, among other valuable possessions, Sciabas and her beautiful child. After various adventures their vessel got separated from its convoy, and was attacked by six Maltese cruisers. Headed by the Aga, the Mohammedans made a gallant resistance; but their master being killed by a cannon-ball, they surrendered at discretion. When the Maltese boarded their prize, their cupidity was gratified by the richness of the cargo; they found Sciabas dead, apparently of fright, and her handsome little boy playing about, unconscious of the danger of his situation. Surprised by his beauty, and the magnificence of his garb, they inquired as to his parentage, and their captives, hoping probably to obtain better treatment for themselves if they exaggerated the value of the prize, declared that the child was Sultan Ibrahim's eldest son, whom they were escorting to Mecca, to have him circumcised. The victors greedily swallowed this tale, and, delighted with their good fortune, set sail for Malta, where they no sooner arrived than they noised abroad the capture they had made of the Grand Sultana and the Sultan's eldest son. The joyful intelligence was spread through all Christendom, and caused such excitement that portraits of the mother and child were extensively sold all over Europe. So highly was their prize valued, that the Knights of St. John talked of proposing the return of the Isle of Rhodes, which had been won from their enfeebled grasp by the Turks, as a ransom for the child and its mother; for they concealed the fact that she was dead, and substituted a slave in her stead. Letters were sent to Ibrahim to inform him of the capture of his wife and child; but as a long time elapsed and he vouchsafed no reply, the Maltese began to question the identity and value of their little captive, who, in the meantime, had been treated with regal attention. Finally, in 1649, they were enabled to make positive inquiries in Constantinople, by means of a certain

Master Pietro, who knew Turkish; and were intensely chagrined to learn that the Grand Sultana and her eldest boy were both comfortably located in the Mohammedan capital, whence, indeed, they had never departed. This intelligence caused the grandees of Malta to treat their youthful charge with less consideration; but as they did not desire to become the laughing-stock of Europe, they concealed the truth, and allowed the world to remain in ignorance of it. As for the son of Sciabas, he was christened with the name of Ottoman, and consigned to a monastery in Italy. When the young Turk grew up, he was treated with no slight amount of consideration by many persons who believed in his royal parentage, and as " Father Ottoman " was considered a shining light by his fellow Dominicans.

MAHOMET BEY, PRETENDED TURKISH PRINCE.

A.D. 1668.

IN 1668 a work appeared in France, with a license from the King, to whom it was dedicated, bearing for title, *Histoire de Mahomet Bey, ou de Jean Michel Cigale, Prince du Sang Ottoman, Basha et Plénipotentaire Souverain de Jerusalem, du Royaume de Cypre, de Trebizonde,* etc. This work, which purported to contain the veritable adventures of its author, was the production of a man declaring himself to be descended from the illustrious Cigalas of Sicily, and who cited several passages from various authors to prove that his family had intermarried with most of the royal families of Europe. His own immediate parentage was ascribed to Scipio, son of that famous Viscount Cigala who was taken prisoner by the Turks in 1561, just after Andrew Doria's grand victory over them. Scipio, having been captured with his father, according to this book's account was taken to Constantinople, and in order to ingratiate himself with the Sultan, Solyman the Magnificent, adopted Mohammedanism, and was rewarded with the post of generalissimo of the army, and the hand of a royal princess. Mahomet Bey, said the veritable history, was the result of this illustrious alliance. Having received a princely education, Mahomet, according to his book, was made Viceroy of Palestine; and whilst in the Holy Land was so impressed by a miraculous vision that he determined to become a Christian, and abandoned the intention he had of pillaging the Holy Sepulchre at Jerusalem. Obliged for the present to disguise his conversion, he was advanced to the governorship of the Isle of Cyprus, and made general of the army destined for the conquest of Candia. During the two following years he contrived to hear mass, befriend and deliver several Christians from slavery, and perform various notable deeds, of which, strange to say, no one had heard until he published this wonderful book. The Sultan now assigned to him the sovereignty of Babylon, Caramania, Magnesia, and numerous other provinces; but on his way to take possession of his new domains he was favoured with another miraculous vision, of a very singular character, which thoroughly confirmed him in his Christianity. Other marvels followed; but the Jesuit dying to whom he had confided his idea of renouncing his high duties and becoming a Christian, his public renunciation had to be deferred. Returning to Constantinople, he was compelled to accept the Viceroyalty of Trebizond, and the Governor-Generalship of the Black Sea. On arrival at his new post, he collected all his valuables and confided them to an envoy named Chamonsi, with instructions to carry them into Moldavia, and there await his employer's arrival, he having determined to abandon the Mohammedan territory and faith at the same time. Betrayed and robbed by his faithless messenger, he was set upon by a party deputed by the Governor of Moldavia to seize him; but after having performed prodigies of valour, only equalled by those of Baron Münchausen, he succeeded in killing all his assailants, and escaping in the borrowed garb of a peasant.

Reduced from his princely rank to the condition of a penniless wanderer, but still bent on becoming a professed Christian, Mahomet crossed the frontiers and made his way to the Cossacks, then at war with Russia. In the Cossack army, runs his tale, he discovered three soldiers whom he had released from captivity in former times. These men recognized their deliverer, and making known his quality to their chiefs, he was treated with respect, and invited to honour their country by receiving baptism in it. But Mahomet had resolved to make his profession of the Christian faith in the city of Rome, and to receive the sacrament from the Pope's own hands. On learning this resolve, the Cossacks, who were schismatics, became so unfriendly that he was forced to fly their country, and take refuge in Poland. There he received a very kindly reception from the Queen, Maria Gonzaga, and became so impressed with her friendliness that he yielded to her persuasions, and was baptized by the name of John in the Cathedral of Warsaw. From Poland, according to his own story, he proceeded to Rome, where the Pope no sooner heard of his arrival than he gave him audience; and having heard his adventures, bestowed his apostolic benediction upon him. Still influenced by the kindness of the Polish Queen, he returned to Warsaw, deviating somewhat from the way, however, in order to assist the Emperor of Germany against the Turks. To display his zeal for Christianity, Mahomet tells his readers he encountered and slew the Turkish general in single combat, and performed such feats of daring, that had we not his own testimony for their truthfulness, they would not be deemed credible.

The great things he had done for the German Emperor procured for him from that potentate the post of guardian-captain of his artillery, but that was not a sufficient inducement to retain him at Vienna; so, peace being concluded, he departed for

Sicily, to find out some of his relatives and their allies. As a scion of the illustrious house of Cigala, he was received with royal honours by the Viceroy of the island, as he was later on by the Viceroy of Naples, according to his own veracious story. After being fêted by the nobility of this latter kingdom he revisited Rome, and was highly honoured by the new Pope, Clement the Ninth, who introduced him to everybody of note. After various adventures he finally reached Paris, where the King and chief members of the Court exerted themselves to the utmost in order to pay him every respect and attention. A palace was provided for him, and when he left the country chains of gold and medallions of the King and Queen were presented to him.

Such is the history of the life and adventures of Mahomet Bey as detailed by himself. A very different account is that given of him by John Evelyn, author of the *Diary*, and other patient investigators. According to their story, this pretended member of the chief royal families of Europe was the son of an opulent citizen of Trogovisti, a town of Wallachia. Prince Matthias, of Moldavia, who had held the claimant's father in much esteem, when he died took his son into his service, and sent him on a mission to Constantinople. When he returned home an honourable career was open to him, but he took to such disreputable courses that, had he not been warned in time to take to flight, he would probably have ended his adventures on the gallows. A second visit to Constantinople, this time as a fugitive from justice, did not improve his morality. He resided in the Turkish capital until the death of Prince Matthias, when he returned to Wallachia; but receiving unequivocal proofs that his past offences were not forgotten, he deemed it prudent to retire once more to Constantinople, where he renounced Christianity for the usual pecuniary recompense. Unable to make much progress with the Turks, or finding the neighbourhood growing too hot to be pleasant, he started on his travels through Christendom. By pretending that he had resigned his Mohammedan honours in order to embrace Christianity, this *soi disant* scion of the Ottoman royal family often obtained aid and protection from various dupes. Finally he came to England, and presented a copy of his mythical history to the King. For some time he was received at Court, but eventually some high personage who had seen him at Vienna, and knew something of his true history, exposed his imposture. The last that is known of this pretender is that he was drawing an annual pension from the imperial treasures at Vienna in his old character of a Mohammedan prince converted to Christianity.

THE FALSE HERCULES D'ESTE OF MODENA.

A.D. 1747.

IN 1747 a young man of elegant appearance arrived at Rochelle, in France. He was accompanied by an elderly person, who, from his studious care of his young companion, appeared to be his tutor. They took apartments in a quiet house, and furnished them in a moderate manner at their own expense. The avowed object of their visit to this French seaport was to procure a passage for the younger of the two to some foreign port; but owing to the difficulty of evading the English cruisers —the two nations then being at war with each other— it was a long time before a vessel would put to sea. Ultimately, a passage was taken on board a small merchantman bound for Martinique, and the youth and man prepared to embark. When leaving his apartments, the landlady enquired what was to be done with the furniture, and was told, with a gracious smile, by the younger of the twain, to keep it as a souvenir of him.

The elderly personage then parted from his young companion, who embarked on board the West Indian merchantman, whither his reputation had, apparently, preceded him. Instinctively the captain and crew recognized the fact that they had an important personage on board, and therefore did all that they could to let him see they knew it. The elder man, who had taken a passage for the youth, had vouchsafed no further information to the captain than that his passenger was a person of distinction, whose friends would one day gratefully repay any attention paid to him; but that was sufficient to procure him every attention. At one time he was enabled to do the crew a service, which certainly increased their respect for him. Alarmed by English cruisers, nearly all the crew had taken to the shallop, and had hurried off so quickly that no provisions had been taken with them; consequently they were soon starving. The young passenger, however, purchased a quantity of refreshments from a native boat that came out to them, and shared it equally amongst all on board. They got back safely to their ship, but the youth was taken with an illness, during which he repaid their anxious inquiries and attentions more with a courteous hauteur than with gratitude. He appeared to shrink from all familiarity, but, as it was necessary that he should have an attendant during his illness, he selected a young sailor of about his own age, named Rhodez, who was respectably connected, and fairly well educated. Rhodez, with whom the youthful stranger became somewhat more confiding than he had been with the others, stated that their passenger was Count de Tarnaud, son of a field-marshal; but this scarcely satisfied the inquisitive, who grew more mystified daily as they beheld the great deference with which the confidant treated the interesting invalid.

On arrival off Martinique, the port was found to be too strictly blockaded by the English cruisers to be entered; and, to save themselves from capture, all had to take to the boats, and by abandoning their ship and cargo, contrived to land safely, but destitute. The supposed count did not appear much grieved at his misfortune, but, attended by Rhodez, at once put up at the best establishment he could discover. The attentions of his host, Ferrol, he accepted as a matter of course, and behaved with such mysterious assumption of grandeur, that the household at once put him down as a prince in disguise. Rhodez could not, or would not, afford any further information than is already known, which it may be well imagined had been thoroughly circulated through the place by the Count's fellow-passengers. Rumours spread rapidly, and at last attained such dimensions that the commandant of the port thought it high time to make the mysterious stranger's personal acquaintance. He invited the *soi disant* count to his house, and his invitation was accepted. Attended by the useful Rhodez, the unknown removed to the commandant's dwelling, and by a certain incident at the very first meal he partook of there, contrived to impress his new host with an idea of his importance. On sitting down to dine, he found that he required a handkerchief, whereupon Rhodez got up and brought him one. This surprised the company present, as at that time, as Rhodez knew well, it was not only unusual, but even considered dishonourable, for one white man to wait upon another. Whilst everybody was in a state of perplexity at this incident, a note from Ferrol was handed to the commandant, wherein it stated: "You wish for information relative to the passenger who lodged with me for some days; his signature will furnish more than I am able to give. I enclose you a letter I have just received from him." This letter, written in a schoolboy hand and badly worded, contained a few words of thanks for Ferrol's services, and was signed " Este," and not Tarnaud. Here was more mystery. All kinds of persons and books were consulted in order to solve the enigma; and at last, by means of an almanac, the youthful stranger was identified as Hercules Renaud D'Este, hereditary Prince of Modena, and brother of the Duchess de Penthièvre. This discovery, which was substantiated by the testimony of two officers of somewhat shady reputation, but who were reputed to have seen the young prince in Europe, was quickly noised about, and the stranger's health was drunk to a full accompaniment of all his supposed titles. The *soi disant* "count" appeared to be extremely annoyed at this discovery, having, so it seemed, signed the note with his real name inadvertently; and although he did not deny the rank imputed to him, the disclosure appeared to excite his haughty displeasure.

After a time, becoming accustomed to the loyal recognition of the people, the supposed prince interested himself warmly in the interests of the natives. Owing to the strict blockade maintained by the English, supplies from the neighbouring islands became scarcer and dearer; and, to make matters worse, had to be obtained through the intervention of certain monopolists, of whom the Marquis de Caylus, the Governor of the Windward Islands himself, was the chief. The Commandant at Martinique, who hated the Marquis, sided with the people in their murmurs, and sought to interest his princely guest in their complaints. The youthful scion of royalty declared himself indignant against the monopolists, and swore to put an end to their exactions; which being duly reported, rendered him more popular than ever.

News of all these things coming to the Governor's ears, he began to grow uneasy, and, to judge for himself, invited the "Count de Tarnaud" to visit him; but received for answer, that although to the rest of the world the stranger might be the Count de Tarnaud, to the Marquis de Caylus he was Hercules Renaud d'Este. "If he desires to see me," said his highness, "let him repair to Fort Royal, which is half way, and in four or five days I shall be there." At first the Governor was so impressed by this imperative style, and the reports which his emissaries brought him, that he started for Fort Royal, but growing sceptical, he retraced his steps. Not finding him at the appointed place, "the prince," attended by quite a retinue of gentlemen, proceeded to Fort St. Pierre, where the Governor beheld him from a window, and exclaiming that he was the exact image of his royal mother and sister, left the place in a panic and repaired to Fort Royal.

After this his "highness" threw off all further reserve, assumed the honours of his position, appointed a household and a suite of attendants, and accepted, without reserve, the generous hospitality of the inhabitants. As might be expected from his youth and exalted birth, he never denied himself the gratification of a whim, and joined in all the maddening dissipation of the place. One remarkable thing was noticed, and that was, that whatever frolic or excess he joined in he never forgot his dignity of prince, and so continued to command the respect of his companions. At first he must have suffered much inconvenience from the fact that although hospitably entertained from the moment of his arrival, he had landed in the island without a coin in his pocket; but his good fortune soon remedied this defect. The Duke de Penthièvre had a large property in the island, and his agent, hearing of the awkward position in which the young prince, his employer's brother-in-law, was placed, very friendlily put the funds in hand at his disposal. His highness graciously accepted this useful offer, and henceforward was enabled to pay his way with royal regularity.

During this period of almost absolute power, the prince had written home to his family, whilst the Marquis de Caylus sent a special messenger to Europe to detail what had happened, and to ask for instructions. Meanwhile peace was proclaimed, the blockade raised, and prices returned to their normal condition. By this time the youthful visitor, having contrived to spend fifty thousand crowns of the Penthièvre funds, and strained the hospitality of the islanders to its extreme limits, deemed it time to depart. Accordingly, attended by all his household and the royal physician, he hoisted an admiral's flag on board a merchant vessel, and, under a royal salute from the fort, set sail for Portugal. Scarcely had their expensive guest departed before a courier arrived with an order for the stranger's arrest, whilst the agent of the Penthièvre family learnt, to his dismay, that he would be expected, for his want of caution, to make good half of what he had allowed the *soi disant* prince to cheat him out of.

Meanwhile, the young adventurer arrived at Faro, in Portugal, and landed amid an artillery salute. He requested a courier should be sent at once to Madrid, as also conveyance for himself and suite to Seville. Everything was placed at his disposal, and, on his arrival at the latter city, which he entered in triumphantlike style, he began a life of festivity similar to that he had carried on in the West Indies. Still provided with funds, he entertained right royally all those who fêted him in return, and speedily won the admiration of the women and the envy of the men. In the midst of all this festivity, an order arrived for the prince's arrest! He was lodging with the Dominicans, who, after a time, despite the indignation of the populace, agreed to give him up, provided no blood were shed. At first the officers found it difficult to execute this agreement, the youth, who was a good swordsman, making it a dangerous task to approach him; but ultimately he was secured by stratagem, and thrown into a dungeon. The following day, for some inexplicable reason, he was released from his fetters, and placed in the best apartment the prison afforded. The "prince," who haughtily refused to answer any questions, was finally condemned to the galleys; and his retinue, upon a charge of a supposititious nature, were expelled the Spanish dominions.

Upon the prisoner's removal to Cadiz, great military precautions were taken, as it was feared a riot on his behalf might be made. On arrival at Cadiz, he was consigned to Fort de la Caragna, and the commandant was instructed to treat him, the convict, with politeness! Being allowed liberties not often granted to prisoners, he availed himself of an opportunity to escape, and got on board an English vessel. On arrival at Gibraltar, the captain reported to the governor that he had on board a personage claiming to be the Prince of Modena. "Let him beware of landing," responded the governor, "for I shall have him apprehended immediately!" The bewildered captain informed his "highness" of the reply, and his passenger, warned by the past, remained on board. The vessel departed with this claimant to royalty, of whose further proceedings history makes no mention.

CHARLOTTE, PRINCESS OF RUSSIA.

A.D. 1752.

THE Czarovitch Alexis, son of Peter the Great of Russia, was married in October 1711, at Torgau, to the Princess Charlotte of Brunswick. In July of the following year, being then only eighteen years of age, the young bride made her public entry into St. Petersburg. She is always described as an amiable and beautiful girl, and was, so it is averred, the choice of Alexis himself. Be this as it may, there can be no doubt that the Czarovitch treated his youthful consort with neglect, even if he did not brutally ill-use her; some authorities, indeed, asserting that he frequently struck her, although, as she was liked and protected by the Czar, his father, of whom he stood in considerable dread, this scarcely seems probable. Alexis gave up his time to the society of a favourite girl of the lowest extraction, and amid various kinds of debauchery forgot or ignored the existence of his wife, and the two children she bore him, one of whom, a daughter, died in childhood; whilst the other, a son, ultimately became Peter the Second.

Some ascribe the intense antipathy Alexis appeared to entertain for his unfortunate wife to a belief he entertained that she complained of him to the Czar, who frequently, and in no very measured terms, took occasion to expostulate with him on his conduct to his wife.

Soon after the birth of her second child the Princess grew dangerously ill, and her malady was heightened by the deep melancholia which had for some time past preyed upon her. It was soon seen that her case was hopeless; and every one, save the Princess herself, and her abandoned husband, appeared to be deeply affected. Alexis never came near his dying wife, whilst the poor Princess herself appeared to be only too willing to escape from the miseries of life. She seemed to anticipate death as a merciful release from her troubles, and implored the physicians not to torment her any longer, as she was resolved to die.

On the day before her death she dictated a document addressed to the Czar, in which she left all the funeral arrangements to him, and recommended both her children to his care and affection, so that they "might be educated according to their birth and position." Her jewels and valuables she left to her children; her dresses to her cousin and dear companion, the Princess of Courland; requested that her debts might be discharged, and the expenses of those who had accompanied her to Russia defrayed home. She thanked the Czar and his wife Catherine for their kindness to her, and, in fact, left arrangements for all her worldly matters. On the following day, November 1st, 1715, she died, and, despite the fact that she died in the Lutheran faith, although she had been strongly solicited to abjure it for the Greek Church, out of respect for her memory the Czar had her remains interred with regal pomp in the Cathedral Church of St. Peter and St. Paul at St. Petersburg.

The foregoing particulars have been thus minutely given in order that the great improbability of the story told by the adventuress who subsequently assumed her name and rank might be rendered the more manifest. According to the story told by a woman who appeared in France about the middle of the last century, and claimed to be the deceased Princess Charlotte, the Princess, soon after the birth of her son, taking advantage of the Czar's absence from his capital, caused a report of her death to be circulated. The Czarovitch, who not having paid any attention to her when alive, was scarcely likely to give himself much trouble about her dead, was averred to have ordered the body to be buried without delay; whereupon, according to the claimant's statement, a piece of wood was substituted for the supposed corpse, and was interred within the Cathedral, whilst the Princess made good her escape into France.

A woman who had resigned her home and infant children in order to avoid the worry of a husband's neglect or brutality, would be expected to return to her father's home; but this princess, it is alleged, first made good her retreat to France, and then, still apprehensive of discovery, notwithstanding the fact of the burial of her supposed remains, embarked for the United States, and settled in Louisiana. There she met a French sergeant who had formerly been in St. Petersburg, and all unregardful of her royal birth, married him, and bore him a daughter. In 1752, this *ci devant* princess, accompanied by her French husband, visited Paris, and as she was walking in the Tuileries was seen and recognized, after all those years of change, by Marshal Saxe, who, however, gallantly promised not to betray her secret, and kindly procured a commission for her husband in the Isle of Bourbon, whither the strangely assorted couple went. Having lost her second husband and her child, the doubly bereaved princess returned to Paris in 1754, in the company of a negress. Getting into difficulties, in consequence of the East India Company refusing the bills she had brought with her in her husband's name, through her inability to prove herself to have been his wife, she took the opportunity of revealing her real rank to a gentleman who had known her in the Isle of Bourbon and, consequently, was induced to offer her his assistance. Soon after this wonderful revelation the *soi disant* princess disappeared, but it was supposed that she had retired to the court of her nephew, the Duke of Brunswick. The King of France, it was averred, had long known the whole circumstances, and had even enjoined the Governor of the Isle of Bourbon to pay her the honours due to her rank. He also, it is said, sent an account of the discovery in his own handwriting to Maria Theresa, the Empress, who immediately wrote to the supposed princess, her aunt, and, doubtless, thinking a woman who had abandoned one husband and family would not be more particular over the next, advised her to quit her present husband and child, whom the King of France promised to provide for, and come and reside in Vienna. This female claimant seems to have utterly disappeared after the bill transaction in Paris, but her story, told in a dozen different ways, may be read in the histories and memoirs of the last century.

THE FALSE PETER THE THIRD OF RUSSIA.

A.D. 1773.

THE history of Russia has already furnished our records with some remarkable cases of pseudo royalty in the tragic stories of the Demetriuses and others, the suspicious circumstances so frequently attendant upon the death of members of the royal family of the Romanoffs having, doubtless, been the means of engendering such impostures as herein detailed. Yet the mystery surrounding the death of Peter the Third was not very dense, scarcely any one doubting that he was murdered at the instigation of his consort, Catherine the Second.

Well acquainted with the use schemers made of hasty and private interments, the Empress determined that the body of her deceased husband, upon whose vacated throne she was installed, should be publicly exposed in accordance with ancient observances, notwithstanding the circumstances of his death. The corpse was conveyed to the capital, and bedecked with his well-known Holstein uniform, Peter the Third's remains were placed in the Church of St. Alexander Newsky, and for three days the people were permitted to take their last view of their murdered monarch. The appearance of the exhibited body is said to have confirmed the spectators in their idea that the unfortunate Czar had been assassinated, whilst the forethought of the Empress was quite ineffectual in preventing impostors personating the deceased sovereign. Soon after Peter's death rumours were circulated to the effect that he had escaped from the hands of his intended assassins, and was living in an obscure part of the country in close concealment. In consequence of these reports six several false Peters, with stories more or less plausible, arose to excite insurrections amongst the discontented people. Five of these impostors were easily disposed of, and without any great loss of life; but the rebellions excited by the sixth shook the Empire to its foundations, and caused a frightful effusion of blood and treasure. Pugatchef, this sixth and last claimant, was the son of a poor Cossack, and as a private soldier had served some years in the Russian army. At the siege of Bender, in 1769, his extraordinary likeness to Peter the Third had been much noticed, one officer observing, "If the Emperor, my master, were not dead, I should believe that I saw him once more." He was of larger make and far greater vigour than Peter, but otherwise the resemblance was great, as may be seen by comparing the portraits in the British Museum of the Czar and the rebel. Having deserted from the army, and taken refuge amongst some religious sectaries of the Cossacks of the Ural, Pugatchef, acquiring the support of these discontented fanatics, boldly announced that he was Peter the Third himself, that he had escaped from the daggers of the assassins, and that the story of his death was an invention of his enemies. In September 1773, he raised the standard of revolt, and having some military skill and experience, combined with personal activity and courage, and a perfect knowledge of the country, he was enabled to entirely defeat the small force sent against him. This success swelled his band into an army, and brought many skilled soldiers, especially discontented Poles, to his aid. Combining religious impositions with his regal one, he tricked the populace into receiving him as their benefactor, and as the supporter of the Church, as well as their Czar. Force after force that was sent against him was defeated, until even Moscow trembled before his approach; and had he boldly marched upon the capital, the probability is that it must have succumbed, and the imperial power would have been completely overthrown.

He established a court, adopted the insignia of the empire, conferred patents of nobility, and issued gold, silver, and copper coins, bearing his image, and the inscription: "Peter the Third, Emperor of all the Russias." But as the adventurer became powerful, he cast off the mask, and dissipated the confidence of his followers by his debauchery and contempt for religious observances. His natural ferocity, no longer under curb, was exercised upon his opponents, whom he mercilessly massacred without respect to sex or age.

Catherine and her advisers, no longer able to treat this rebellion as the marauding expedition of a gang of robbers, were compelled to make the most strenuous efforts to meet the impostor's forces. An army of veterans, chiefly recalled from the Turkish campaign (then being prosecuted), and numbering forty-five thousand men, aided by a formidable train of artillery, took the field under the command of an experienced general. Proclamations were issued, offering a pardon to all who returned to their allegiance, and proffering a reward of one hundred thousand silver roubles for the person of Pugatchef, alive or dead. The pretender, in return, circulated manifestoes, in which he abolished servitude, freed unconditionally all the serfs, and created them proprietors of the soil which they tilled.

This was an attack upon the empire's weakest point; and had the insurgent leader been as prudent as he was daring, he might easily have overturned the existing government.

During the spring of 1774, victory, followed by the most terrible excesses, hovered between the two opposing powers, until at last Palitzin, the imperial general, completely routed Pugatchef, and drove him into the fastnesses of the Ural mountains. Just as the Empress and her courtiers were congratulating themselves upon the supposed annihilation of the rebellion, however, the claimant reappeared with recruited strength, and again obtained many successes. Again was he routed and driven back, and again did he return with fresh armies to renewed victories. Once more repulsed, he was still enabled, for the fourth time, to gather together fresh legions of insurgents, who seemed to spring into being at his call. But his strength was nearly spent; his experienced men had been destroyed; his new recruits were ill-armed and untrained serfs, whilst peace with Turkey enabled the Empress to concentrate all her strength for a crushing blow. Pugatchef advanced along the banks of the Volga towards Moscow, committing the most terrible atrocities at the various places he captured. Aware that the late Czar, whom he still personified, spoke German, he carefully executed any of his prisoners who owned to a knowledge of that language. Finally, surprised by the Imperial troops, his hordes were routed with great slaughter, and he himself narrowly escaped by swimming across the Volga, and gaining the almost inaccessible steppes of the Ural. Attended by three followers only, he lurked about for some time, until at last betrayed and handed over to a Russian general. Sent to Moscow, he was tried with all possible formality, condemned, and executed on January 21st, 1775, having previously, according to official report, confessed his real name, and been recognized by his relatives. Thus ended one of the most daring impostures on record, after having cost the empire upwards of a year's panic and confusion, an enormous loss of property, and, worse than all, the sacrifice of at least three hundred and fifty thousand lives.

CASPAR HAUSER, "THE HEREDITARY PRINCE OF BADEN."

A.D. 1828—33.

NO more innocent claimant to royalty, nor more undeserved a victim, than was Caspar Hauser, is told of in history. His birth, his death, and his real parentage, are all enveloped in a mystery no amount of research has, as yet, been able to pierce. The world first heard of him on Whit-Monday, the 26th of May, 1828. On the afternoon of that day a citizen of Nuremberg was interested in the appearance of a youth in a peasant's dress, who seemed endeavouring to walk into the town, but with unsteady gait and tottering step. When approached and accosted, he replied in the Bavarian idiom, "I want to be a trooper as my father was," and held out a letter addressed to the captain of the fourth squadron of the sixth regiment of Bavarian Light Horse. As this officer was quartered near the citizen's own house, he assisted the crippled lad to the place indicated. The captain was from home, and as the bearer of the letter to him appeared to be little better than an idiot, and incapable of giving other account of himself than that he wanted to be a trooper as his father had been, he was conducted to the stable and given some straw, upon which he laid himself down and fell asleep. When the captain came home the lad was sought for, but it required no little exertion to awaken him. He could not give any account of himself, and recourse was had to the letter for an explanation. It was written in German, in an unknown hand, and expressed a wish that the youth should be admitted into the captain's troop of Light Horse. A memorandum in Latin was enclosed, and was stated by the writer of the letter to have been received by him on the 7th of October, 1812, when the present bearer, then a baby, had been left at his house. It proceeded to declare that the writer was a poor labourer, and the father of ten children; but that he had complied with the unknown mother's request by bringing up the little foundling secretly, and by giving him instructions in reading, writing, and Christianity. This communication contained neither the writer's name nor address, nor did the memorandum enclosed throw much light on the subject.

It ran thus:—" The child is already baptized; you must give him a surname yourself; you must educate the child. His father was one of the Light

Horse. When he is seventeen years old, send him to Nuremberg to the sixth regiment of the Light Horse, for there his father was. He was born on the 30th April, 1812. I am a poor girl, and cannot support him. His father is dead."

This unsatisfactory communication, and the utter inability of the youth to furnish any account of himself, determined the captain to have nothing to do in the matter; so he immediately handed his charge over to the police. Taken to the guard-room, a close examination was made of the strange arrival. His attire consisted of a coarse shirt, pantaloons, and a peasant's jacket, in which was a white handkerchief marked "K. H." (Kaspar Hauser). He was of medium height, broad-shouldered, and well built; his skin was white and fine, his limbs delicately moulded, and his hands small and beautifully formed. The soles of his feet were as soft as the palms of his hands, and were covered with blisters, which seemed to account for his difficulty in walking. But subsequent investigation offered further elucidation upon this point; it showed that his feet had never before been compressed by shoes, and that owing to the confined position in which the unfortunate boy had been retained, the joint at the knees, instead of being a protuberance when the leg was straightened, formed a hole or depression. Whilst under examination he manifested neither dread nor astonishment, but continued to cry and point to his feet. His behaviour excited the compassion of the officials, and one of them offered him some meat and beer; but he rejected them with disgust, partaking, however, of bread and water with apparent relish.

The usual interrogations were put to him, as to his name, whence he came, and his travelling pass; but all in vain. Beyond his frequently repeated expression, "I want to be a trooper as my father was," little could be got out of him. Some of the spectators began to fancy the lad was playing a part, and their suspicions were increased when, upon writing materials being offered to him, he took a pen, and slowly and clearly wrote " Kaspar Hauser." Unable to make out whether he was an idiot or an impostor, he was removed to a tower near the guard-house, where rogues and vagabonds were confined. Given a straw bed, he lay down and slept soundly.

Although at first utterly unable to furnish any account of himself, Caspar, under the kind and judicious treatment of his keepers, gradually learnt to speak, and gather some idea of the world and its ways. As soon as ever he was really enabled to communicate with those around him, the Burgermeister, Herr Binder, went to visit him, and take down his deposition. From what the poor lad then or subsequently stated, the following extraordinary particulars were recorded, and are, or were some few years ago, still preserved in the Nuremberg Police Court. Caspar's account was to the effect that he did not know who he was, or whence he came; that as far back as he could recollect he had always lived in a hole or cage, and always sat upon the ground, with his back supported in an erect position,—a statement which the condition of his knees fully corroborated. He had been kept in a state of semi-darkness in this subterranean place, clad only in shirt and trousers, and fed only upon bread and water. At times he had been overpowered with heavy sleep, and on awakening from this state would find his nails trimmed, his clothes changed, and his dungeon cleaned out. Every day a man, whose face he had never seen, would come and bring him a loaf of bread and a pitcher of water. Some time before Caspar's removal into the outer world, "the man" was accustomed to come every day with a small table or board, which he put over the lad's feet, and putting a sheet of paper upon it, guided his hand, in which he had placed a pencil, so that he gradually learnt to write. By constant imitation of the marks or lines "the man" guided him into making, Caspar Hauser had learnt to make the letters composing his own name, or rather the name he went by. This writing appears to have greatly delighted the poor captive and, beyond two wooden horses, would seem to be all that he had to amuse himself with. At last "the man" came one night, lifted Caspar on to his shoulders, and taking him out of the dungeon, carried him towards Nuremberg. He made the lad try to walk, but the unusual exercise caused him such pain that he fainted; and when he recovered his senses he found himself alone by the city gates, where he was discovered.

Everything appeared to corroborate this most extraordinary circumstance; it was some time before he could walk without stumbling; he appeared to have no control over his limbs; the attempt to compress his feet into boots caused him great torture, whilst walking drew sighs and groans from him. His eyes, unaccustomed to the light, became inflamed; he had no idea of the relative distances of things, and when he first saw the flame of a candle was so delighted that he put his finger into it. When pretended thrusts were made at him he exhibited no alarm, and did not recoil, and altogether showed such intense ignorance of the operations of the senses that those about him were convinced that he was no impostor, as strangers imagined him to be. The meanwhile, whilst the lad was gradually becoming reconciled to the wonders of the world around him, the strange story of his discovery was spreading rapidly all over Europe. The scientific and the curious flocked to Nuremberg in order to behold this human phenomenon, and presented him with toys and gifts. But he complained that his visitors teased him, and that he had headaches, which he never had when he was in his cell. At this time, the close scrutiny which his story underwent began to excite curious suspicions as to the facts of his parentage. It was argued that a mother desirous of getting her child adopted was not likely to have placed it at the door of a poor labourer already burdened with ten children of his own, and with the hope that he could support it for seventeen years; nor was it within the bounds of probability that a man so situated could have kept the boy all that period without putting him to work. Moreover, what reason could the labourer have had for keeping the boy concealed all that time? The mother might have wished concealment, but certainly not the adopting labourer. It was felt there was some deep mystery behind all this secrecy, and everything about it pointed to a noble origin for Caspar.

These ideas, and the rumours they generated,

had tragic consequences for the poor lad. On the 17th October, feeling unwell, he was excused from a mathematical class he attended, and was allowed to stay at home. A little after noon, whilst a woman in the house was sweeping, she noticed blood spots and bloody footmarks, and following them to the cellar, there found Caspar, apparently dead, and with a dreadful wound across his forehead. Medical assistance was procured, and the lad removed to his bed. After a time he recovered from his insensibility, but for a long while was in a state of delirium, during which he frequently murmured, " Man come —don't kill me—I love all men—do no one anything. Man, I love you too. Don't kill—why man kill?"

The poor innocent lad was carefully tended, and as soon as he had regained sufficient strength to be interrogated a judicial inquiry was made into the affair. According to the victim's account, "the man" had entered the house, and as he was softly treading along a passage Caspar noticed that he was masked, but before he could make any further observation he was felled to the ground by the wound in his forehead, and became insensible. He could not explain how he got into the cellar, but fancied he must have crawled there in a half-insensible condition. Nothing resulted from the judicial inquiry beyond the fact that the extraordinary case excited more comment than ever. Among others who became interested in the strange matter was Earl Stanhope, then in Germany. This English nobleman was so pleased with the lad's amiable ways and his misfortunes, that he placed him in the care of an able tutor. After a time Caspar received the appointment of Clerk to the Registrar's Court of Appeal, and performed his duties so well that Lord Stanhope spoke of adopting him and taking him to England. This probably induced his powerful foes to put him out of the way at once. On the evening of the 14th December, 1833, as Caspar was returning home from his official duties, a stranger accosted him, and by a promise of revealing his parentage inveigled him into the palace gardens, where he plunged a dagger into his side, and then instantly disappeared. Caspar just managed to get home and murmur a few words when he became insensible, and before the police arrived he expired.

The police appear to have made great efforts to discover the assassin, but without success. The King of Bavaria caused an inquiry into Caspar Hauser's case to be made, and the well-known jurist, Feuerbach, to whom the inquiry was deputed, reported significantly, " *There are circles of human society into which the arm of justice dares not penetrate.*"

Who then was Caspar Hauser, and why include him among pretenders to royal lineage? It was surmised, and still is believed by many, that he was elder son of the Grand Duke Karl of Baden and his much-admired consort, the Grand Duchess Stephanie Tascher, Napoleon's adopted daughter. Their son, born in September 1812, was alleged to have died when a few weeks old, but the popular idea in Baden was, and indeed still is, that this boy was carried off and a dead child substituted in his stead, at the instigation of the Grand Duke Karl's uncle and successor, Ludwig, a man to whom the most disgraceful crimes and cruel outrages are imputed.

THE FALSE DAUPHINS IN FRANCE.

1793—1859.

HAD not these pages already proved to what an extent human credulity could go, it would be almost useless to offer the following most extraordinary details as matters of fact. That a dead person might be personated by a living being is quite within the range of probability, but that thirty or more totally different individuals should in this nineteenth century not only deem it, but prove it, possible to dupe numbers of people into believing that they were a prince whose decease had been publicly certified and most zealously investigated into, scarcely seems to come within the range of the possible. In order to better comprehend the various marvellous stories detailed by the impostors about to be referred to, the true story of the little dauphin, styled by the French royalists Louis the Seventeenth, should be told.

On the 27th March, 1785, Louis Charles, the second son of Louis the Sixteenth of France, was born at the Château de Versailles. The birth of this second son caused great rejoicings in the royal circle, where his earliest years were environed with all the care and adulation bestowed upon princes. His father created the child Duke of Normandy, whilst the death of his elder brother in 1789 brought him next in succession to the throne, raised him to the rank of dauphin, and, if possible, made him a greater idol than before in the eyes of the Court. At four years of age he is described as of slight but well-shaped figure, with a broad, open forehead, finely-arched eyebrows, and large blue eyes; his complexion was fair, and his hair, of a dark chestnut colour, curled naturally, and fell in ringlets over his shoulders. Amid the gaieties of the French Court at Versailles doubtless the little lad's mental faculties were rapidly developed, although it would be idle to place any credence in the authenticity of the sage replies and clever repartees ascribed to him by some Court writers. But his happy childish life was of short duration: the starving and infuriated populace of Paris, driven from one misery to another, deemed if they could only bring the king to the metropolis means would be discovered for overcoming their distress. Under the influence of this infatuation, an enormous crowd, chiefly composed of women, marched from Paris, invaded the regal precincts of Versailles, and deputed a few of their number to see the king.

Louis the Sixteenth received the deputation with great kindness, but the power of royal words was over, and the following day he was compelled to return to the capital, accompanied by the Queen and the dauphin. The people, in their destitute condition, could only think of bread, and believing the king could command possession of it, familiarly styled him "The Baker," so that now, seeing the royal family's return, they shouted joyously, "No more poverty; we are bringing back the baker and his wife, and the little shopboy." The poor child so designated could not find anything better to say of the Tuileries, as they entered that place, than, "Everything is very ugly here." His mother endeavoured to console the prince for that by reminding him Louis the Fourteenth had lived there.

It is needless to recapitulate the well-known story of the precarious state to which the royal family were speedily reduced in Paris, and how they made secret preparations for leaving the capital in disguise. On the 20th of June, 1791, the attempted flight was commenced, the dauphin, who had been dressed as a girl, deeming he was being attired to play in a comedy. The flight was, indeed, carried out, but the royal party got no further than Varennes, where they were discovered, and after being allowed to spend the night there were carried back to Paris (although it was wonderful that they reached it alive), and five days after their departure were again installed in the Tuileries. From that time until the 13th of August, 1792, when the royal family were imprisoned in the Temple, the whole of its members had been under close surveillance, and had no fresh opportunity of escaping from the capital. From the date of their incarceration in the Temple their doom was sealed, and nothing but death released any one save the Princess Marie Theresa from captivity. After a while the king was separated from his family, and placed in a portion of the prison called the Great Tower, and there also the dauphin was placed, with his father, until the trial and execution of the latter, when he was returned to his mother's care. On the 3rd of July, 1793, a most terrible trial awaited the hapless boy: on that day, in accordance with a decree of the "Committee of Public Safety," he was removed from the custody of his mother, and consigned to the charge of Simon, formerly a cobbler, but now appointed guardian to the dauphin at a salary of twenty pounds a month, conditionally upon his never leaving his youthful prisoner, and never, upon any pretence, leaving the tower where the child was confined.

The fearful and miserable life which the poor boy

endured whilst in charge of the brutal Simon, and his scarcely less brutal wife, is so well known that the saddening details need not be repeated; suffice to recall the fact that by hard work, strong drinks, close confinement, improper food, and even blows, the unfortunate child was brought to the brink of the grave. M. de Beauchesne, to whom the world is chiefly indebted for the harrowing story of Louis the Seventeenth's wretched fate, has, it is to be hoped, overdrawn the terrible picture; but, after making every allowance for royalist exaggeration, enough of horror remains to excite the pity of the hardest hearted. Brutal and debasing as was Simon's regimen, it was not rapid enough in its process to satisfy "the Committee of Public Safety;" they, therefore, dismissed him from his post, and made different arrangements. For the future the poor innocent little victim was confined in one room, into which his coarse food was passed through a wicket, and from which he was never permitted to emerge either for exercise or fresh air. "He had a room to walk in, and a bed to lie upon; he had bread and water, and linen, and clothes, but he had neither fire nor candle." For months this system of solitary confinement was endured by the child, who, reduced to a state of helpless stupidity, no longer attempted to change his linen, or cleanse himself, and was allowed to drift into a condition of utter imbecility. Ultimately an improvement was effected in the little captive's condition, and under the better treatment accorded him he rallied for some time; but the cruelty he had endured had been too certain in its operation to allow of any permanent restoration to health. In the month of May, 1795, his jailers reported to the Government that "little Capet was dangerously ill." A physician was sent to attend on the child, but his prescriptions were no longer of any use. On the 8th of June he told one of his keepers, "I have something to tell you!" but the man waited in vain for the revelation, for whilst he listened the poor child's life had passed away.

When the dauphin died he was ten years and two months old. The members of the Committee of Public Safety having concluded their day's sitting when the news was brought, it was deemed advisable to conceal the event until the morrow. Supper was prepared for the child as usual, and Gomin, his attendant, took it up to the room. Many years afterwards this man stated that when he entered the apartment he went to the bed and gazed upon the corpse of the little dauphin. "His eyes, which while suffering had half-closed," he relates, "were now open, and shone as pure as the blue heaven, and his beautiful fair hair, which had not been cut for two months, fell like a frame round his face." The next morning four medical men came to examine the body, and make their report, which they did in somewhat ambiguous terms, stating that at the Temple on a bed in a room of the second floor of the Tower they had seen "the dead body of a child, apparently about ten years old, which the commissaries declared to be that of the late Louis Capet's son, and which two of our number recognized as that of the child they had been attending for several days." About twenty soldiers, however, who are stated to have known the "little Capet" by sight when at the Tuileries, were also admitted, at their own request, to view the body of the child, and signed an attestation to the effect that they recognized it. The body was finally put into a coffin, and on the 10th of June, 1795, was taken to the cemetery of Sainte Marguerite, by the Rue St. Bernard, and buried in an unknown spot, which to this day no one has been enabled to find out.

M. de Beauchesne, to whose indefatigable industry the public is almost entirely indebted for what is known of the little dauphin's prison life, is our chief authority for the preceding details. His very circumstantial and affecting account is corroborated by official documents of undeniable authenticity, and to every unprejudiced mind must carry the conviction that the unfortunate " Louis the Seventeenth " died, how, when, and where, we have already described.

THE FALSE DAUPHINS: JEAN MARIE HERVAGAULT.

ALTHOUGH the unfortunate dauphin's death had been officially certified to by so many persons, the secret manner of his burial afforded full scope for the propagators of strange rumours to exercise their talents. The circulation amid provincial cliques of baseless reports of the prince having made good his escape from the Temple, and of another child having been substituted in his place, was not unlikely to meet the ears of those able and willing to avail themselves of the popular myth; it is not, therefore, so phenomenal that some impostors sought to pass themselves off as the deceased dauphin; but the large number of different individuals who made the attempt is, probably, unparalleled in all history. Out of the thirty, according to the computation of M. de Beauchesne, claimants to the name of this luckless scion of royalty, it will be only requisite to furnish accounts of the most notorious. The first of the pretenders, in order of time, was Jean Marie Hervagault, the putative son of a poor Normandy tailor. He was born at St. Lô on the 20th of September, 1781.

His mother had been a pretty woman, and scandal had connected her name somewhat closely with that of the Duke de Valentinois. Young Hervagault had a delicate complexion, fair hair curling naturally, an agreeable countenance, and dignified manners that would not have discredited the child of royalty. When he was twelve years of age he set off on his travels, and after having duped several persons by pretending to be a son of different members of the aristocracy, he determined to, or was persuaded to, take upon himself the name of the little prince, "Louis the Seventeenth." According to the story given by his adherents, or accomplices, the dauphin had not died in the Temple as was commonly supposed, but had been carried forth in a basket of soiled linen, and the scrofulous and idiotic child of the tailor Hervagault left in his stead. The pseudo Louis the Seventeenth had not made much progress in his first essay before he was arrested as a vagabond, and sent to Cherbourg. There his father reclaimed him, and he was allowed to go free under parental care. Some few years later he recommenced his imposture, and being again arrested was sentenced at Châlons-sur-Marne to a month's detention. Not deterred by this, he began his old tricks again, and being speedily captured was condemned to two years' imprisonment. Finally, he was caught the next time at Vitry, practising his favourite imposture and living at the expense of his dupes. On this occasion the pretended prince was favoured with four years of detention. These successive rebuffs did not deter Hervagault from pursuing his game upon the next opportunity. When for the last time he presented himself before the judge, his easy assurance and dignified mien greatly impressed the court. The large and influential crowd of his dupes, who were spectators of his trial, remained firm believers in his case, and would not be dissuaded from their belief by the most positive proofs as to the falsity of his tale. Men of exalted position and wealthy persons accorded him their sympathetic aid, and considered themselves well paid for whatever they might do if "the dauphin" condescended to honour them with a bow, or if they were permitted to kiss his royal hand. The imperial police, however, would not stand much nonsense, and shut up the youthful claimant in the asylum of Bicêtre, as an incorrigible lunatic. Hervagault now and for henceforth disappeared from public gaze, but the vacant dauphinship was speedily claimed by Jersat, an old soldier; and upon his being disposed of, Fontolive, a mason at Lyons, started as a claimant for the honours. He in his turn vanished from the scene, and then Bruneau aspired to the title.

THE FALSE DAUPHINS: MATHURIN BRUNEAU.

MATHURIN BRUNEAU was the son of a maker of wooden shoes, and was born at Vezin, in the department of the Marne-et-Loire. By his eleventh year the precocious rogue had already endeavoured to palm himself off as a nobleman's son, and encouraged, apparently, by the facility with which his claims were acknowledged, he determined to fly at a higher game, ultimately giving forth that he was the Duke of Normandy. Although this impostor never was anything but a vulgar peasant, devoid of education and good manners, he acquired a large following, and really became a source of danger to the Government. In 1817, that is to say, in the early days of the Bourbon restoration, when the throne was in a very precarious condition, this claimant, taking advantage of a famine and the general discontent, had placards posted on the walls and public places of Rouen, denouncing the reigning monarch, Louis the Eighteenth, claiming the crown for himself as the legitimate son of Louis the Sixteenth, and promising, if placed on the throne, to reduce the price of bread to three sous per pound. The long wars of the empire had exhausted France, and reduced the provinces to such a condition of misery that any inflammatory leader was likely to obtain a large retinue of discontented followers, so that even so mean and insignificant a personage as Bruneau was, was dangerous.

Bruneau, according to the minute and circumstantial investigation which Monsieur Verdière made into the past events of his life, had undergone a series of adventures as surprising as those of Gil Blas, and had perpetrated a variety of deceptions of a most extraordinary nature, culminating in his grand assumption of the *rôle* of the dauphin, the titular "Louis the Seventeenth." When this ridiculous pretender, who had already undergone imprisonment as a rogue and an *imbecile*, first attempted to take upon himself the royal title, he was attired, says his historian, in nothing but a nankin vest, linen trousers, and a cotton cap, stockingless and moneyless,—not even a claimant was ever in worse condition. According to the best account, this absurd impostor was first prompted to assume the dauphin's name at the suggestion of an eating-house keeper of Pont-de-Cé, who had formerly been cook to Louis the Sixteenth.

Orders were issued for the arrest of the audacious pretender, but he did not wait for them to be put into execution. He decamped, and was traced to St. Malo, and arrested there. He was so illiterate that he could neither read nor write; but for all that he caused a letter to be written to the King, Louis the Eighteenth, in which, under the title of the Dauphin, he reclaimed his paternal heritage. Sent to Bicêtre, in January 1816, Bruneau did not suffer himself to be cast down. In his leisure hours he employed himself at his juvenile occupation of making wooden shoes; but with an eye to future opportunities he endeavoured to make proselytes to his regal pretensions. Among his companions in misery he discovered some very useful converts or accomplices, including Larcher, a pretended priest; Tourly, a forger; the Abbé Matouillet; Branzon, condemned for robbery; and other equally respectable associates. The rumour was speedily noised abroad that "Louis the Seventeenth" was at Bicêtre, and visitors continually came to see "the unfortunate prince," and leave him substantial proofs of their devotion and sympathy. They raised a civil list for him, overwhelmed him with unsolicited gifts, wrote the "Mémoires du Prince," and eventually made so great a stir in the city that the judicial authorities were compelled to interfere, and on the 10th of

February, 1818, had Bruneau up before the Police Tribunal. The accused presented himself in his invariable cotton cap; and mean, illiterate, and miserable as was his appearance, was saluted by a few faint cries of " *Vive Louis the Seventeenth!*" What the man wanted in dignity he made up for with assurance; and although Monsieur Dossier, the Procureur du Roi, with pitiless severity disclosed the whole of the impostor's past career, the insolent vagabond contested to the end of his cross-examination that he was the veritable Duke of Normandy. His vulgarity, his contradictions, and his whole demeanour were so palpable, it is wonderful that a single person could have been duped. And yet numerous people, many of them holding respectable positions in society, permitted themselves to be fooled, and even subscribed large sums of money for the pretender's support. The money which had been subscribed for this *soi disant* " Louis the Seventeenth " had been chiefly deposited at the Bank of France—a fact of which the prosecution was, of course, aware,—and therefore the judges did not content themselves with condemning Bruneau to five years' imprisonment for his imposture, and a further term of two years, to commence at the expiration of the five, for his insolent behaviour during his trial, but they also sentenced him to a fine of three thousand francs, to be paid to the Government, and to defray three-quarters of the cost of his prosecution, to meet which penalties the moneys standing to his credit at the bank were confiscated. It was also ordered that at the expiration of his term of imprisonment Bruneau should remain at the disposal of the Government, to determine what was thought fit as to his future. Bruneau's accomplice in the fraud was sentenced to two years' imprisonment, and the payment of one-fourth of the cost of the prosecution. Bruneau died in prison.

THE FALSE DAUPHINS: HÉBERT.

HITHERTO the claimants to the dignities and name of the deceased Dauphin were persons of low origin, and with little or no pretensions to education. But the next pretender to be introduced was of aristocratic appearance, talented, and furnished with a plausible story to account for his past life. His first appearance before the public as a claimant, so far as history is cognizant of his adventures, was on the 12th of April, 1818, when a young man was arrested by the Austrian police, near Mantua, for styling himself Louis Charles de Bourbon. He declared himself to be French, and said that he was travelling for his education, the truth or falsity of which assertions did not trouble the police, but the surname of "De Bourbon" did, and they demanded an explanation. The arrested traveller declined to respond to their interrogations; but desired that a communication which he had addressed *A Sa Majesté Impériale seule* should be forwarded to the Emperor.

From this communication, and other documents found in the prisoner's possession, it was discovered that he claimed to be Louis Charles de Bourbon, Duke of Normandy, and the legitimate heir to the crown of France. This illustrious captive was sent to Milan, and, without undergoing the formality of a trial, was promptly incarcerated. His story, as fully detailed in the "*Mémoires du Duc de Normandie, fils de Louis XVI., écrits et publié par lui-même,*" at Paris in 1831, and subsequently republished with modifications and additions in 1850, is of a most interesting character, and is evidently as veracious as most of those issued by his contemporary rival claimants. According to the Milan prisoner, whose memory, unlike that of most of the pretenders to the dauphin's name, was clear as to the miseries he had endured during captivity in the Temple, after the death of Marie Antoinette, the wife of his jailer Simon consented to aid his escape, having been bought by the gold of the Duke de Condé, who had sent two faithful emissaries, the Count de Frotté, and Ojardias, a pretended physician, to Paris, in hopes of rescuing the royal child. The name of Ojardias, it is as well to remark, notwithstanding the important part he was called upon to play in this drama, has entirely escaped the researches of all historians contemporary or recent, and appears only in the pages of this remarkable narrative. This pretended physician, having purchased the co-operation of Madame Simon, and secured for himself, by unrecounted means, the post of medical adviser to the dauphin, counselled the invalid prince should be permitted a little exercise, and recommended a wooden horse for that purpose.

The prison officials, who were in league with Ojardias, and ceded everything to Madame Simon, consented to the proposed new treatment being tried; the pretended physician therefore had a wooden horse manufactured large enough to contain a child of the dauphin's size. Simon, who was annoyed at having to resign his functions, and disgusted at not being awarded any indemnity, was speedily talked over by his wife to aid the escape of the prince, or at all events consented not to offer any obstacle to his evasion. The date fixed for the attempted escape was the 19th January, 1794, on which day Simon had to resign his guardianship. Everything being prepared, and Simon gone to take a parting glass with the prison officials, his wife, according to her daily custom, conducted the little prince to a lower room. In a few moments Ojardias arrived with the horse designed for the dauphin's exercise. This new toy really contained in its interior a child of about the same height as the prince, but dumb, and suffering from a scrofulous complaint. This unfortunate boy, who had been attired in clothing similar to the dauphin's, had partaken of a strong narcotic, and was consequently in a profound slumber. The exercise horse was conspicuously displayed before the prison officials, who, never having read of the stratagem by which Troy was taken, or their vigilance having been lulled by the pretended doctor's gold, did not find it necessary to inspect it too minutely. No sooner was Ojardias left alone with the dauphin than he extricated the sleeping mute from his prison-place and deposited him on the chair recently occupied by the prince. Rapidly explaining to little Louis what his purpose was, he rolled him up in a bundle of linen Madame Simon had prepared for departure, and proposed to that good lady, who was superintending the dismantling of her rooms, that he should help her downstairs with the said bundle. The jailer's wife feigned that she could not allow the doctor to do anything of the kind, nevertheless permitted him to carry off the precious burden, whilst she took occasion to inveigh pointedly against the nonchalance of some men, who would let a poor woman work herself to death without stirring a finger to help her. Meanwhile Ojardias, accompanied by Simon, descended with the bundle, and deposited it on the cart waiting to carry off the goods of the ex-jailer, and which was immediately driven off. On the same day that the dauphin, according to the

Milan prisoner's account, had been rescued from the Temple, Simon, in vacating his post, handed over the substituted child to the commissioners delegated by the commune to replace the ex-jailer. The child was still in a deep sleep, and the commissioners had no motive for awakening it, as they had no suspicion as to its identity. They listened to Simon's declaration, and certified on his affidavit that "the young Capet had been remitted to them in good health."

Such was the story given by this claimant to account for his escape from the Temple; but such is the unfortunate habit of these pretenders, in a subsequent account he materially altered the narrative, and instead of being taken away in a bundle of linen, averred that he had been removed in the toy horse itself, which Simon's wife made Ojardias carry downstairs again after he had effected the exchange of children, notwithstanding the remonstrance of some of the officials, under the pretext that she would not have it brought into the room without her husband's consent, and he, when appealed to, refused to allow of its being introduced.

Resuming the story, as given in the *Mémoires*, we read, that when the dauphin was removed from his very confined place of imprisonment he was cleansed, purified from the unpleasantness of his Temple captivity, and then put to bed. In the evening he was aroused, removed, and placed in another artificial horse, but this time it was of life size. In the interior of this animal, which in the company of two real horses was harnessed to a cart filled with straw, were placed every convenience and comfort for the rescued prince. This horse was covered with real skin, and in every respect made to imitate a living animal, so that the officers appointed to inspect all passing vehicles were in no way suspectful of the deception, and permitted the conveyance and its precious freight to pass without hindrance, so that the little Duke of Normandy, after all his troubles and mishaps, arrived safely in Belgium, and was delivered into the hands of the Prince de Condé.

Unfortunately De Condé, instead of at once proclaiming the rescue of his youthful king, kept the whole affair mysteriously private, and secretly sent the boy to General Kléber, of all persons in the world! The revolutionary general accepted the strange trust reposed in him by his opponent, and passing off the scion of royalty as his nephew, Monsieur Louis, took him to Egypt with him. Bonaparte was strangely disquieted at the sight of this youth, in whom he foresaw a rival; but the prince was once more carried away, and confided to the care of another republican general, Desaix! This officer made the royal shuttlecock his *aide-de-*

camp, and took him with him to Italy. After the battle of Marengo the dauphin revisited France, and instead of seeking any of his family's adherents, confided his secret to Lucien Bonaparte, and to Fouché, Napoleon's Minister of the Police. Certainly an eccentric youth, and one whom it was a great waste of time to have rescued from the Temple precincts! Fouché introduced the young prince to Josephine, and the Empress at once recognized him from the scar below the right eye, which Simon had caused with a serviette. Unfortunately for his peace in France, the young man took part in Moreau's conspiracy, and Pichegru's paper having revealed to Napoleon the fact that Desaix's *aide-de-camp* was none other than the Duke of Normandy, the youthful conspirator had to fly, and, like most of his rivals for the title of dauphin, took refuge in the United States.

The adventures of this claimant in the New World are too marvellous for our pages; and as he prudently suppressed the account of them in the second issue of his *Mémoires*, it is not necessary to allude to them any further. In 1815, according to his story, he returned to France, determined to reclaim his rights. His former protector, the Prince de Condé, at once recognized him in private, and introduced him, by means of a curious stratagem, to his sister, the

Duchess d'Angoulême. The princess, however, regarding the dauphin as the enemy of her family, because of the terrible avowals which Simon had wrung from him in the Temple, refused to have anything to do with him. Flying from this cruel reception, the repulsed brother, so he averred, had travelled through many foreign lands, including England, when, happening to visit Italy, he was arrested and thrown into prison in the way already narrated.

Thanks to Silvio Pellico's charming prison records, this pretender's story can be continued, and in a more truthful fashion. In the same prison of Ste. Marguerite, where the Italian author was confined, was also held in durance vile the *soi disant* Duke of Normandy. The two captives became acquainted, and the Frenchman, by this time probably grown a half believer in his own imposture, declaimed so strongly against his "uncle," Louis the Eighteenth, the usurper of his rights, that Pellico appears to have been partly converted, whilst the jailers were quite convinced of the authenticity of the prisoner's claims. These guardians of the cells had seen so many changes of fortune during the last few years, that it appeared to them by no means improbable that one day their "royal" captive might leave his prison for a throne; having this belief in view, they granted the pretender everything available save freedom.

In 1825, the Austrians, deeming, doubtless, his "Royal Highness" had had sufficient time to disabuse himself of his belief, released him after a captivity of more than six years and a half. The pretender took himself off to Switzerland, where he made some dupes; and in 1826 re-entered France. Grown prudent, however, he concealed his royalty under the name of Hébert, and under that cognomen obtained employment in the Préfecture of Rouen. As Colonel Gustave he appeared in Paris, in 1827, and in the following year reasserted his rights, as the following communication addressed to the Chamber of Peers shows:—

"LUXEMBOURG, 2 *February*, 1828.

"NOBLE PEERS,—Organs of justice, it is to your exalted wisdom that the unfortunate Louis Charles de Bourbon, Duke of Normandy, confides his interests. Saved, as by a miracle, from the hands of his ferocious assassins, and after having languished for several years in various countries of the globe, he addresses himself to your noble lordships.

"He does not reclaim the throne of his father; it belongs to the nation, which alone possesses the right to dispose of it. He only demands from your justice an asylum for his head—which he cannot repose anywhere without peril—and in a country which more than thirty years of exile have not caused him to forget.

"THE DUKE OF NORMANDY."

The only apparent result of this appeal was the proposition made by Baron Mounier to the Chamber, that for the future no petition should be received of which the petitioner's signature had not been legally recognized, and which was not presented by a peer.

Meanwhile his "Royal Highness" was carefully sought for in Belgium and Holland, although he was all the time concealed in Paris. He managed during this epoch to pick up a number of anecdotes and incidents appertaining to the captivity of the royal family in the Temple, and by displaying the ever useful cicatrice over his right eye, and the traces on his knees and wrists of the malady contracted during his slavery under Simon, was enabled to gather together a faithful band of believers, who assisted him to the full length of their purses. Among other items of testimony, he declared that he had visited Madame Simon on her death-bed at the Hospital of Incurables, where she did really die on the 10th June, 1819, and that she instantly recognized him and wept tears of pity. What, however, he pointed to as the strongest proof of his royalty was the fact, he alleged, that every one who could have testified to his identity had been suddenly put out of the way. He carefully, in fact, utilized the names of such persons as he had been acquainted with during his life, and whose decease had been in any way sudden, or not fully explained. As, for instance, beginning with the famous surgeon Desault, to whose care the dauphin had been entrusted, and who had expired suddenly on the 4th of June, 1795, he intimated that he had been poisoned, because he imprudently declined to accept the substituted dumb child as the veritable Duke of Normandy. In a similar way he accounted for the deaths of several well-known personages whose lives he asserted had been sacrificed on his behalf. He even went to the extent of asserting that Louis the Eighteenth knew well that he was the veritable dauphin, and that when warmly expostulated with by his nephew, the Duke de Berry, for concealing the fact from the world, had not only excused himself by saying, " Do you not comprehend that this recognition has become impossible, as it would render all existing treaties invalid and imperil the general peace ?" but had even added significantly, " Take care of yourself, Berry !" And within a fortnight De Berry fell beneath the attack of Louvel.

These accounts of those who had suffered for their lawful king, although they may have convinced his credulous dupes, did not render it particularly safe for the claimant to put himself near the minions of the French police; he therefore found it prudent to keep himself concealed, and change his *noms de guerre* at intervals. The revolution of 1830 afforded him, however, a fair opportunity for the display of his talents. No sooner was a provisional government established than the claimant, now concealing his royalty under the title of the Baron de Richemont, addressed a demand to it that his rights should be observed, whilst he protested against the proclamation of the new "king of the French," as Louis Philippe was designated. The pretender also published the following letter, which was, he averred, a copy of one he had addressed to the Duchess D'Angoulême:—

"The time has now arrived, Madame, when, abjuring sentiments which nature and humanity alike disavow, you should give to my case the explanation necessary for putting an end to the ills that have oppressed me for so many years. I will not reproach you; your position imposes a religious silence upon me; but mine—have you considered it?

"If your heart is still able to understand the plaintive cry of outraged nature; if more than thirty-six years of suffering and exile would appear to you sufficient punishment for the enormous crime of being your nearest relation; if your hate is extinguished, break this culpable silence; since fortune once more puts you at the mercy of foreigners, would it not be better to throw yourself into the arms of your unfortunate brother?

"LOUIS CHARLES."

Notwithstanding this appeal, the princess did not seek out the persevering claimant, although the police did, and on the 29th August, 1833, succeeded in arresting him. He refused to give his name, but the act of accusation styled him Ethelbert Louis Hector Alfred, calling himself "Baron de Richemont." His real name, however, was supposed to be Hébert, as in all affairs of importance he had borne that, although he had used a variety of others. Among the witnesses called was Andryane, who had been a fellow-prisoner with the accused in Italy; Lasne, now seventy-four, who had been a personal attendant on the dauphin in the Temple, and who testified that he was well acquainted with the person of the little prince, who had died in his arms, although two strangers had been to his house to vainly try and persuade him that the child had been changed; the Duke de Choiseul, who, when interrogated by the prisoner, acknowledged that certain words ascribed to Marie Antoinette had been overheard by him; the Duke de Caraman remembered that an intriguing individual named Ojardias had brought to Thiers a sickly child, that for the moment passed for the dauphin; whilst Monsieur Rémusat, a medical man, deposed that Simon's widow, who died in a hospital in 1815, had told him that the dauphin was not dead.

On this slender fabric the *soi disant* "Duke of Normandy" based his case, and with much dignity, and real or happily simulated emotion, recounted the story the reader is already acquainted with. At times his audience did not fail to manifest interest and sympathy in his recital. When the prosecution had spoken, and his advocate had presented the defence, the claimant said with calm dignity: "The Advocate-General has told you that I am not the son of Louis the Sixteenth; does he tell you who I am? I have formally requested him to do so, but he preserves silence. Gentlemen, you will appreciate this silence, as also the cause which hinders us from producing our titles. This is neither the place nor the time. Competent tribunals will have to decree what is needed in that respect. You have been informed that inquiries have been made everywhere, but the Advocate-General is very careful not to let you know the result: he is not able to, his power does not extend so far as that, because another power forbids it. And what, gentlemen, would you think if, with a man like me, and at such a moment, they had neglected to carry out their investigations in the places where I have sojourned, and notably at Milan! No, no, gentlemen, do not believe but that they have written everywhere, and everywhere have obtained that which they asked for, that which they dare not make known to you. If I am in error, it is in the best faith; unfortunately, I have been in this belief for about fifty years, and I see well that I shall bear this error with me to the grave."

Ultimately the Court, whilst acquitting Hébert of roguery and conspiracy, found him guilty of sedition, and he was sentenced to twelve years of detention. He listened to his sentence without manifesting any emotion, and in retiring said, " He who does not know how to suffer is not worthy of the honour of persecution!" In 1835 Hébert contrived to escape from prison, in company with two other captives, and succeeded in getting out of France. For some years this pretender contented himself with urging his claims from abroad, and with re-issuing revised and enlarged editions of his *Mémoires*, still sustained by the credulity of his dupes; but in 1848, protected by the general amnesty, he returned to his native land, and addressed a declaration of his rights to the National Assembly. This proclamation did not appear to excite any public attention, any more than did his declaration of adhesion to the Republic, or the notification of that deed, which he forwarded to the Duchess d'Angoulême, on the 27th of March, 1849.

This claimant, in many respects the most noteworthy of those who aspired to the titles of the unfortunate dauphin, died in 1855, in the little commune of Gleyzé, in the district of Villefranche-sur-Saône, and was interred there on the 10th of August of that year.

THE FALSE DAUPHINS: NÄUNDORFF.

DURING the trial of the *soi disant* Baron de Richemont, the spectators were surprised and amused by a singular declaration addressed to the jury by another pseudo dauphin. This claimant, who varied the old story by styling himself Charles Louis in lieu of Louis Charles, protested that De Richemont was only an impostor put forward in order to confuse public opinion, and stifle the voice of the veritable Duke of Normandy, the author of this document!

This new pretender, if the royalists are to be believed, was a certain Charles William Näundorff, member of a Jewish family of Polish Prussia, and was born in 1775, or ten years earlier than the dauphin. He turned up at Berlin in 1810, and resided there for about two years, earning his livelihood by selling clocks. In 1812 he removed to Spandau, obtained the rights of citizenship, and married the daughter of a Heidelberg pipemaker. He professed to be a Protestant, spoke French with a villainous accent, and yet, in 1825, from some unaccountable reason, gave out to the world that he was the son of Louis the Sixteenth. He had been in many difficulties before he complicated matters by assuming the Duke of Normandy's titles, having been accused of being an incendiary in 1824, and some months later of coining, for which latter offence he was sentenced to three years' detention in the Penitentiary of Brandenburg. On being released from captivity he set up a claim to be the son of Louis the Sixteenth, and actually had the foolhardiness to institute proceedings against the ex-king, Charles the Tenth, and the Duchess d'Angoulême. All he gained by this audacity was an immediate arrest, and expulsion from the frontiers of France, in which country he had taken up his abode. Nothing daunted by this summary action, the pretender appealed to the Council of State, and obtained the services of Monsieur Cremieux to defend his cause, not, it is true, as the son of Louis the Sixteenth, but as a foreigner illegally arrested and expelled. Unsuccessful in his suit, Näundorff passed into England, and continued to play his *rôle* of illused royalty. By these means, and by practising as a spiritualist, the *soi disant* prince contrived to make enough dupes to live by. In 1843 he got into some difficulties with the English police, and being made bankrupt, had to leave the country. Taking refuge in Holland, he expired at Delft, on the 10th of August, 1845.

Unfortunately Näundorff's pretensions did not die with him, for he left two children, Louis and Marie Antoinette "de Bourbon," who some few years since renewed their claims to the reversion of the French throne. In 1873, the son, Louis, summoned the Count de Chambord before a Paris court, to show cause why a judgment pronounced many years ago against Näundorff's father, by the Civil Tribunal of the Seine, should not be reversed in his, Louis's, favour. Notwithstanding the fact that the putative "grandson" of Louis the Sixteenth retained the services of Jules Favre as an advocate, he was unable to soften the iron hearts of the Parisian jury, and had to subside into oblivion.

THE FALSE DAUPHINS : AUGUSTUS MEVES.

OF all the tawdry fictions invented by pretenders to the name and title of " Louis the Seventeenth," none are so ridiculous as the tale told by the Meves family, if that really be their name, and yet none have so persistently troubled the public with printed assertions of their claims as they. The quantum of probability in their story may be gauged by telling it in the words of Augustus Meves, *alias* "Auguste de Bourbon, son of Louis the Seventeenth." However, the tale cannot be given *in extenso* from the works issued by this illustrious man, as, not only has it required several volumes to put it before the world, but it is so contradictory, and at times obscure, that it requires no slight manipulation to render it comprehensible.

Beginning his career with the Temple epoch, this pseudo dauphin, contrary to the accounts of his competitors, declares that he has no recollection of Simon the jailer having ever wilfully ill-treated him, and that owing to a person named Hébert having wounded him in a fit of passion, Madame Simon's womanly feelings were aroused on his behalf, and she determined to save him. His rescue was thus brought about: Tom Paine, author of "The Rights of Man," who was at this time a member of the French National Convention, wrote to a lady friend in London, to bring him a deaf and dumb boy to Paris. This lady, unable to execute the commission, communicated the secret to her bosom friend Mrs. Meves, and she naturally informed her husband. It so happened that Mr. Meves had a son who, being in delicate health, his father was naturally desirous of getting rid of. Mr. Meves, therefore, without confiding in his wife, went to Paris with his son, who, by the way, was neither deaf nor dumb, and placed him in the hands of certain people, who substituted him for the dauphin. The exchange was effected at a time when public interest being concentrated on the Queen's trial, the vigilance at the Temple, says "Auguste de Bourbon," was relaxed. According to the recollection of the dauphin, his escape was thus managed: "It seems to my reflective powers that I was lying on the sofa in the parlour of the small Tower of the Temple, and was awakened by Madame Simon saying, '*Votre père est arrivé.*' She then aroused me from the sofa, taking the pillow therefrom, and putting it into a kind of hamper-basket, and after placing me in it, she covered me with a light dress, and carried the basket across the ground. A coach was waiting at the gate, into which she placed the basket, when we were driven to where Mr. Meves resided. The coach needed to carry Madame Simon's linen disgorged its contents, and in due time the Duke of Normandy was landed in England, where he took the place of Mr. Meves' son, that iron-hearted gentleman having made a vow to Marie Antoinette, whom he contrived to get an interview with, that the young prince should be brought up in utter ignorance of his true origin. And that secret," says "Auguste de Bourbon," "he kept to the end of his existence."

Whether Louis Charles so readily forgot his real parents and position does not, probably, need investigation. He was placed at a day-school, where after a fashion he learnt English, and, subsequently, at a boarding-school at Wandsworth. Meanwhile, Mrs. Meves having discovered that her son had had to take the place of young Louis in the Temple, very naturally wished to effect *his* release. She obtained a deaf and dumb boy, and by a roundabout route took him to Paris. Vigilance being, apparently, again relaxed at the Temple, the unfortunate deaf and dumb scapegoat was now substituted for Augustus Meves, and his escape was effected. "At what precise date this was accomplished," says

"Auguste de Bourbon," "is not definitely fixed, but it is suggested after July 1794. Mrs. Meves did not stay in Paris till its accomplishment (*i.e.*, her son's release), but returned to England in the month of May."

Augustus Meves now disappears from the scene, although it is suggested that he may have been the pretender Näundorff, but the "Dauphin King" was carefully educated by the unnatural parents, who had their adopted child taught the pianoforte. The boy made such progress that an unnamed Scotch newspaper deemed him "only to be equalled by the great Mozart." This success made the foster-father afraid the lad's origin might come to light, so he placed him in the seclusion of a friend's counting-house. His Royal Highness did not admire this occupation, and by Mrs. Meves' aid was enabled to resume his former vocation. He became a volunteer, and joined the "Loyal British Artificers," and in 1811 was promoted to the rank of captain. In 1813 he relinquished the musical profession to become "a speculator at the rotunda of the Bank of England." In 1814 he visited Calais, but the return of Napoleon in 1815 prevented him, says his son, "going to Paris." In this latter year he "observed a lady scrutinising him," at the Old Argyle Rooms, Regent Street, and was informed that it was the Duchess d'Angoulême, the unfortunate victim of all the pseudo dauphins. In 1816 he visited Paris, and found many of the sights quite familiar to his memory. In 1818 Mr. Meves died, and so faithful was he to his promise to Marie Antoinette of keeping the secret of the dauphin's origin, that in his will he absolutely declared the young man to be "his illegitimate son." This naturally aroused the ire of Mrs. Meves, who, bound by no oath, informed her adopted son of his real parentage, declaring somewhat rashly, "Your identity can be proved as positive as the sun at noon-day."

"This disclosure," says "Auguste de Bourbon," "naturally unsettled and perplexed the dauphin, for his early recollections were but vaguely defined." He obtained an order for his putative father's disinterment, but that does not appear to have solved the mystery any more than did the fact that "in 1821 the dauphin became a speculator, and experienced its vicissitudes." In 1823 Mrs. Meves died, after having advised the "dauphin" not to be "induced to read any private memoirs of the queen of France, as it will only set your mind wool-gathering." Unfortunately, Augustus did not follow this prudent advice, and the consequence was that the unfortunate Duchess d'Angoulême was bothered with more fraternal appeals, and with the information that the writer possessed a mole "on the middle of the stomach." Ultimately a French nobleman visited Augustus, and told him that in his opinion the British Government knew who he was, but feared to acknowledge him, as, from the energy of his character, he might put the whole of Europe in a state of fermentation, because, pointed out this Frenchman, "he was not only King of France in right of birth, but also heir to Maria Theresa, Empress of Germany."

On the 9th of May, 1859, this pretender died, but unfortunately his pretensions did not die with him. He left two sons, of whom the elder, known to the public generally as William Meves, has published several ungrammatical and illogical works respecting his alleged royal lineage, under the assumed name of "Auguste de Bourbon."

THE FALSE DAUPHINS: ELEAZAR WILLIAMS.

THE story of this impostor has been a favourite theme with American magazines, some of which, indeed, have sought to throw an air of probability about his pretensions. And, indeed, ridiculous as this pretender's tale may seem, it would be dangerous to aver that it is more absurd than those told by some of his rival claimants to the rank and name of " Louis the Seventeenth." During the years 1853 and 1854, a series of papers on the claims of the Rev. Eleazar Williams to be considered as the deceased dauphin were published in *Putnam's Magazine*, and in the latter year the Rev. J. H. Hanson published a work entitled " The Lost Prince," purporting to contain " Facts tending to prove the identity of Louis the Seventeenth of France and the Rev. Eleazar Williams, Missionary to the Indians."

In order to account for the strangeness of the story told, the biographer carries his records back to 1795, when a family styling themselves De Jardin are said to have arrived in Albany from France. The family consisted of a Madame de

Jardin, who appeared to be a personage of some distinction, and a man who passed as this lady's husband, but really appeared to be her servant, from the deferential manner in which he treated her; and two children, a boy and a girl. There appeared to be a considerable amount of mystery connected with these children, or at all events with the boy, who was about ten years of age, was always alluded to as " Monsieur Louis," and in whom visitors had no difficulty in discovering a resemblance to portraits of the French royal family. Madame de Jardin acknowledged that she had been maid of honour to Marie Antoinette, and still retained in her possession several relics of her unfortunate mistress. The De Jardins did not inform their neighbours what had brought them to Albany, and, what was still more tantalizing, they suddenly departed without saying why they went away.

The next episode, although showing no very clear connection with the De Jardin mystery, is suggestively allocated with it as its sequel. It tells how, later in the year 1795, two French strangers, having with them a sickly boy of about ten years of age, visited the Iroquois settlement at Ticonderoga, near Lake George. This boy was left in charge of Thomas Williams, a chief of the Iroquois settlement, who adopted him and brought him up in the same way as his own eight children, giving him the name of Lazar, the Iroquois equivalent for Eleazar. All went smoothly for three or four years, during which period Eleazar, who was little better than an imbecile, forgot his French, and remembered little or nothing of the past. Some few incidents of a noteworthy character, however, occurred. One day two strangers visited the settlement, and whilst one stood aside the other met Eleazar, and embraced him, and shed a plenteous supply of tears over him. He talked a good deal to Eleazar, but as he spoke French, and the boy only understood Iroquois, they could not derive much information from one another. The next day the Frenchman repeated his visit, examined Eleazar's knees and ankles, wept more tears, and, what seemed to him more reasonable, presented him with a piece of gold before he went away.

Probably the most important event, however, that happened to him during his stay at the Indian settlement occurred when he was supposed to be about fourteen. Up to that period he had been not far removed from an idiot, when having been accidentally struck on the head by a stone, his intelligence and memory were suddenly restored. Eleazar now recalled to mind visions of the past, especially recollecting a beautiful lady, attired in a splendid dress with train, and who had been accustomed to take him on her knees and play with him. Other reminiscences of a less pleasing nature were called to mind, including the figure of a threatening, ignoble, and terrible man, undoubtedly that of Simon; for when a portrait of the infamous cobbler was shown to Eleazar, he recognised it with horror.

One night Eleazar overheard a conversation between his reputed parents which revealed to him the fact that he was not their own, but only their adopted, child; but the circumstances did not, apparently, make any strong impression upon his mind, as he soon forgot it until after events recalled it. Eventually, he was sent to school at a village in Massachusetts, in the company of John, one of his reputed brothers. John could not be done much with, and returned to his Indian life, but Eleazar made good progress in his studies, became very devout, and acquired the cognomen of "the plausible boy."

Years passed by, and "the plausible boy" became a plausible man, in his time playing many parts, some of which were scarcely worthy of the descendant of a hundred kings, or even of a Christian missionary, which was the *rôle* he now chiefly assumed. Sometimes he was an Indian chieftain, sometimes a military spy; at one time one thing, at another time another; but through all, as he firmly believed, and as his countenance betrayed, and as the marks on his body testified, he was "the Lost Prince," the dauphin who was supposed to have perished in the Temple. If he had had any doubts left on this matter, they were all removed, according to his own account (and numbers of his faithful adherents believed in him implicitly), in October 1841, in an interview he had with the Prince de Joinville, who chanced to be travelling in the United States that year. According to the account furnished by the Rev. Eleazar Williams, who by this time appears to have taken to the missionary avocation permanently, he happened to be on board the same steamer as the French prince, who after having made inquiries about him of the captain, requested the honour of an interview. This Eleazar affably granted, and De Joinville was brought to him. "I was sitting at the time on a barrel," says plausible Eleazar; "the prince not only started with evident and involuntary surprise when he saw me, but there was great agitation in his face and manner—a slight paleness and a quivering of the lips—which I could not help remarking at the time, but which struck me more forcibly afterwards . . . by contrast with his usual self-possessed manner." After paying Eleazar an amount of respect that quite surprised that plausible priest, and astonished everybody about them, the prince, upon landing at Green Bay, desired the honour of a private conversation with him at the hotel. To this request Eleazar consented, and according to his account, the interview, which was carried on in English, the prince speaking that language fluently, but a little broken, indeed, as did Eleazar himself, yet quite intelligibly, resulted in De Joinville acknowledging that the missionary was indeed the veritable dauphin, the Duke of Normandy, the legitimate heir to the crown of France and Navarre; but requesting him to solemnly resign all his rights and titles in favour of Louis Philippe, upon condition that a princely establishment should be secured to him either in America or France, at his option, and "that Louis Philippe would pledge himself on his part to secure the restoration, or an equivalent for it, of all the private property of the royal family rightfully belonging to me" [*i.e.* Eleazar Williams], "which had been confiscated in France during the revolution, or in any way got into other hands." But Eleazar's ancestral pride was aroused, and after informing De Joinville that he would not be the instrument of bartering away with his own hand the rights pertaining to him by birth, and sacrificing the interests of his family, he concluded by remarking that he could only give the prince the answer which De Provence gave Napoleon's envoy at Warsaw:—"Though I am in poverty and exile, I will not sacrifice my honour!"

Upon receiving this reply the prince loudly accused his guest of ingratitude for thus rejecting the overtures of the king, his father, who, he declared, was only actuated by kindness and pity, as his claim to the French throne rested on an entirely different basis to Eleazar's; that is to say, not that of hereditary descent, but of popular election. "When he spoke in this strain," avers Eleazar, "I spoke loud also, and said that as he, by his disclosure, had put me in the position of a superior, I must assume that position, and frankly say that my indignation was stirred by the memory that one of the family of Orleans had imbued his hands in my father's blood, and that another now wished to obtain from me an abdication of the throne." "When I spoke of superiority," says Eleazar, "the prince immediately assumed a respectful attitude, and remained silent for several minutes." On the following day, says "the plausible," he saw the prince again, who, finding his renewed efforts to shake the determination of the dauphin not to resign his hereditary titles were vain, bade him good-bye with the words, "Though we part, I hope we part friends."

Probably the strangest, if not the most ludicrous portion of this story is, that Prince de Joinville deemed it requisite to publicly deny "plausible" Eleazar's little romance, and to declare it to be a tissue of lies from beginning to end, and nothing but "a speculation upon the public credulity."

THE PRETENDED PRINCESS OF CUMBERLAND, ENGLAND.

1866.

OF all the wild stories which have been concocted by pretenders to regal lineage, none that has obtained any public notice has been so utterly absurd in its developments as that told by Lavinia Janneta Horton Ryves. In 1866 this individual, the daughter of Mr. Serres, an artist, and the wife of a Mr. Ryves, actually brought her claim to be recognized as Princess of Cumberland into a court of law. According to the statement which Mrs. Ryves made through her counsel, and which, indeed, was only a recapitulation of what had already appeared in various periodicals, her grandmother Olive had been married to the Duke of Cumberland, brother of George the Third, and had had the marriage acknowledged by that monarch. This statement was supported by several documents purporting to be signed by King George, and several other persons of exalted position, but which were characterized by the prosecution as impudent forgeries, the production, apparently, of

Mrs. Serres, and the jury would seem to have taken the same view of their nature.

The story *in extenso* was this : the Rev. Dr. James Wilmot, of Barton-on-the-Heath, Warwickshire, met and became enamoured of the sister of Count Poniatowski, subsequently King of Poland. Dr. Wilmot married this Polish lady, but, in order to retain his Fellowship, kept the marriage a profound secret. One child, Olive, a very beautiful girl, was the sole issue of this love match. When this lovely daughter was seventeen years of age, she was seen at a nobleman's house by the Duke of Cumberland, fallen in love with, and after a very brief courtship married by the prince. This marriage, which was alleged to have been celebrated by the bride's father, Dr. Wilmot, on March 4th, 1767, was also a secret one. On the 3rd of April, 1772, a daughter, christened after her mother, Olive, was born of this clandestine union; but, previous to the interesting event, the Duke of Cumberland, availing himself of the secrecy of his first marriage, actually committed bigamy by taking unto himself a second wife, in the person of Lady Anne Horton, sister of the infamous Colonel Luttrel. The second Olive, according to the testimony of the claimant, was first baptized as daughter of the Duke of Cumberland, and then, by command of George the Third, in order to preserve her royal father from the penalty of bigamy, was again baptized at another church as the daughter of Robert Wilmot (Dr. Wilmot's brother), and Anna Maria his wife. A certificate to this effect was produced, purporting to be signed by the two Wilmot brothers and the Earl of Warwick, and as means of the child Olive's future identification it was certified that she had "a large mole on the right side, and another crimson mark upon the back near the neck."

The so-called "Princess of Cumberland" died in France, on the 5th of December, 1774, and, according to Dr. Wilmot's supposed certificate, "in the prime of life of a broken heart," evidently caused by her royal husband's desertion of her. George the Third was perfectly cognizant of his brother Cumberland's union with Olive Wilmot, and was therefore deeply indignant at his heartless behaviour; but as, according to another portion of the claimant's story, he had contracted a similar bigamous union himself, he was necessarily compelled to keep quiet about the occurrence. However, in order to compensate his little niece in some way for her loss of birthright, he not only allowed her putative parents five hundred pounds per annum for her support, but placed in their hands the following acknowledgment of her claims to royalty.

"George R.—We hereby are pleased to create

Olive of Cumberland Duchess of Lancaster, and to grant our royal authority for Olive, our said niece, to bear and use the title and arms of Lancaster, should she be in existence at the period of our royal demise.

"Given at our Palace of St. James's, May 17th, 1773.
"CHATHAM,
"J. DUNNING."

When about seventeen this "Duchess of Lancaster" *in petto* came to London, and made the acquaintance of John Thomas Serres, proprietor of the Coburg Theatre, and son of a royal academician. Upon the 1st of September, 1792, this descendant of the sovereigns of England and Poland was married to Mr. Serres, but, as might be anticipated, the union was not a very happy one, and in 1803 a separation took place. Of the four children who were issue of this marriage, two daughters grew up, one of whom, Lavinia, born in 1797, remained with her mother, whilst the other went with her father. Mrs. Serres, who became an author and artist, and published a book to prove that the *Letters of Junius* were written by Dr. James Wilmot, would appear to have been somewhat crazed, at least towards the latter part of her life. She assumed the title of Princess of Cumberland, and brought up her daughter

Lavinia in the belief that she was of royal lineage. Dr. Wilmot, who died in 1807, at the advanced age of eighty-five, was supposed to have left his daughter the following remarkable document:—

"My dear Olive,—As the undoubted heir of Augustus, King of Poland, your rights will find aid of the sovereigns that you are allied to by blood, should the family of your father act unjustly; but may the great Disposer of all things direct otherwise. The Princess of Poland, your grandmother, I made my lawful wife, and I do solemnly attest that you are the last of that illustrious blood. May the Almighty guide you to all your distinctions of birth! Mine has been a life of trial, but not of crime!
"J. Wilmot.
"*January* 1791."

It was not until 1815, according to the evidence given by Mrs. Ryves at the trial, that her mother knew anything of her royal parentage, she having been brought up in the belief that she was the daughter of Robert Wilmot, Dr. Wilmot's brother. When the wonderful information was conveyed to her, through the instrumentality of the Earl of Warwick, she took the title of Princess, and, so said the witness, was even acknowledged by the Duke of Kent and other members of the royal family as a relative. The Duke of Kent, so it was alleged, even granted to the *soi disant* princess one-third of his Canadian estates, binding himself, his heirs, and executors to a solemn observance of the covenant, and promised to see her reinstated in her royal rights. In 1818 he further bound himself, his heirs, executors, and assigns (according to the claimant's story), to pay the Princess Olive an annuity of four hundred pounds; and this annuity, so it was averred, was duly paid until the Duke's demise, after which event it was not continued. Indeed, such trust did the Duke of Kent repose in the "Princess Olive," if the documents produced might be relied on, that he constituted her guardian of his daughter Alexandrina (our present Majesty), and directress of her education, on account of her relationship, and because the Duchess of Kent was not familiar with English modes of education. Out of respect for a mother's feelings, the "Princess Olive," as her daughter explained, did not attempt to execute this desire of her deceased cousin of Kent.

So thoroughly were the "Princess Olive's" royal claims ventilated that, it is averred, she was entertained at the civic banquet at the Guildhall, on the 9th of November, 1820, and permitted, or invited, by the Lord Mayor (Alderman Thorpe), to occupy one of the seats usually assigned to members of the royal family. In 1834 the putative princess, otherwise Mrs. Serres, died, leaving her claims as an inheritance to her daughter Lavinia Jannetta Horton, then the wife of Mr. Anthony Thomas Ryves, and the mother of several children. The personal appearance of Mrs. Ryves, so believers in her claims asserted, was greatly in favour of her alleged descent from the royal family; but, unfortunately for her pretensions, neither judge nor jury would admit such supposed resemblance as evidence.

In replying on the remarkable statements made at the trial, the Attorney-General ruthlessly demolished the whole fabric of the "Cumberland romance." He did not impute aught to Mrs. Ryves more than that having brooded over the matter for so many years she had at last persuaded herself of the truth of the fiction she was representing; but Mrs. Serres, he suggested, was really the concocter of the whole scheme. True it was, contended Sir Roundell Palmer, that the petitioner's mother, Mrs. Serres, was not quite responsible for her actions, so many of them having been of an ultra-eccentric character. He described several of her crazy words and deeds, and showed how she had varied her tale from time to time; at first only claiming to be an illegitimate scion of the royal stock, and first making claims to regal legitimacy in a time of great public agitation

—at the period of Queen Caroline's trial. Indeed, said the Attorney-General, a revolution was threatened by the deceased claimant if her pretensions were not recognized within a few hours.

The jury were unanimous, and immediately pronounced against the claims of the petitioner, Mrs. Ryves, whose wonderful documents and marvellous certificates were all ordered to be impounded. Since that trial, the claims of Mrs. Ryves and her offspring appear to have passed into oblivion.

JOHN SOBIESKI AND CHARLES EDWARD STUART, "COUNTS OF ALBANY," OF ENGLAND.

1847—1880.

THE story of Prince Charles Edward Stuart, the "bonnie Prince Charlie" of song, is too well known to need recapitulation here. That he died in 1788, without leaving any legitimate offspring, is a fact equally well known; as also that his brother Henry Stuart, Cardinal York, who died in 1807, was the last of his ill-fated race. Notwithstanding the incontrovertible nature of these circumstances, attempts have been made within the last thirty or forty years to prove that Prince Charles did leave a legitimate son, the child of his wife the Princess Louisa; and that two brothers, who until quite recently were residing in London under the pseudonyms of "Counts d'Albanie," were the children of this unknown royal prince, and therefore grandchildren of "Charles the Third."

This myth was first publicly propagated in a work entitled "Tales of the Century; or, Sketches of the Romance of History between the years 1746 and

1846," published in 1847, and purporting to be by "John Sobieski and Charles Edward Stuart." Some suggestive hints, it is true, had been thrown out as early as 1822, in a volume of poems by one of these brothers; but that book was published as by "John Hay Allen," and no definite assumption of royal lineage would appear to have been made until the Edinburgh publication of 1847. According to the legend detailed in the three sections into which the work was divided, in 1831 an ancient medical man, of extreme Jacobite views, finding himself dying, confided to a young Highland gentleman, who was visiting him in London, the long-hoarded secret that the Gaels "have yet a king." The young Scotchman is naturally inquisitive as to the meaning of this mysterious communication, and has his curiosity gratified by a recital of the following romantic story by Dr. Beaton.

According to that deceased gentleman, he chanced to be making a tour in Italy, in 1773, and as he was walking along the road from Parma to Florence, he was startled by the passing of a carriage with scarlet outriders. On glancing into the conveyance he was still more startled by beholding the not-to-be-forgotten countenance of his beloved "Prince Charlie," seated by a lady's side. On the evening of the same day, whilst meditating on what he had seen, he was accosted by a man of military appearance, and asked whether he was Dr. Beaton, the Scotch physician. On replying in the affirmative, he was informed that his immediate attendance was required in a case of urgency, and all his questions as to the nature of the patient's malady were disposed of in a very unceremonious manner. His reluctance to be blindfolded before entering a carriage that was in waiting was overcome by the intimation that it was on behalf of him whom both recognised as their royal chief, that is to say, Prince Charles.

After the usual style of such mystic tales, Dr. Beaton was taken to a secluded palace, and after being led through the usual corridors and apartments of such abodes, had his mask removed, and was permitted to inspect the magnificent chamber into which he had been inducted. His conductor did not allow much time for investigation, but rang a silver bell, and his summons being responded to by a little page in scarlet, he was enabled to inform the doctor, after a short conversation in German with the boy, that the accouchement of the lady he had been called in to attend, owing to the absence of her own regular medical attendant, was over, and apparently "without more than exhaustion." The news communicated through so uncustomary a channel was followed by the request that he would render such services as were necessary. He was taken into a gorgeous bedroom, where a lady who spoke English led him towards the bed, wherein he beheld the face of the lady he had seen in the carriage with Prince Charles, whilst by the bedside was a woman holding the newly-born babe wrapped in a mantle. The patient was in a somewhat critical condition, so Dr. Beaton hastily turned to a writing-table near at hand to write a prescription for her, and in so doing beheld among the trinkets on the table a miniature of Prince Charles, attired in the very uniform the doctor had seen him in at Culloden. The lady who had spoken English approached the table as if looking for something, and when Beaton looked again, the portrait had been turned on its face. Having performed his duties, the doctor was persuaded to take an oath on a crucifix, "never to speak of what he had seen, heard, or thought on that night, unless it should be in the service of his king—King Charles;" he was, also, desired to leave Tuscany that night, and then conducted from the dwelling in the same needlessly mysterious manner as he had been taken to it.

The doctor obeyed his injunctions to the letter, and at once departed from the neighbourhood. A few days later he arrived at a certain seaport, and one night, soon after his arrival, he was strolling along the beach when his attention was attracted by an English-looking vessel anchored off the coast. Upon inquiry this proved to be the *Albina*, an English frigate, commanded by Commodore O'Haleran. Whilst he was watching the vessel he beheld a small close carriage, accompanied by a horseman, whom he recognized as his guide on the night he was conducted to the residence of Prince Charles. His curiosity aroused by this singular coincidence, he stopped to watch what happened, and beheld a lady, bearing a babe in her arms, descend from the mysterious vehicle. This lady and her infantile charge were then conveyed on board the frigate, and no sooner had they got on board than the vessel hoisted sail and slowly disappeared. The babe, it is implied, was the legitimate son and heir of Prince Charles, thus mysteriously smuggled off in order to preserve it from the machinations of the English government.

Many years are supposed to have elapsed, and the boy born at St. Rosalie, in 1773, is next introduced as a grown man bearing the name of Captain O'Haleran, and supposed to be the son of the admiral formerly introduced as the commodore of that name. This individual creates no slight sensation in the Highlands by his supposed resemblance to the unforgotten Prince Charlie, whose eagle eye and Stuart features he is said to have; one ancient chieftain, indeed, of somewhat clouded mind, when he beholds the mysterious stranger, who is known by the cognomen of the "Red Eagle," addresses him as "Prince Charles," and reminds his Royal Highness that their last meeting was at the fatal fight of Culloden. Moreover, to make the reader understand the personage's rank beyond all question, his French attendant styles him "Monseigneur," and "Son Altesse Royal." In the final section of this fiction, the "Red Eagle" makes a misalliance by marrying an untitled English lady, and becomes the father, it is natural to infer, of the two individuals whose names figure on the title-page of *Tales of the Century*.

The reader must not imagine that this marvellous romance was intended to be regarded as myth; every effort was made to persuade the public into accepting it as fact, and as fact several persons in Great Britain and abroad have accepted it. But in the *Quarterly Review* for June 1847, the whole story was thoroughly analysed and ruthlessly demolished by some one conversant with all the bearings of the whole case. He undeniably proved that the implied son of Prince Charles was no other than Thomas, younger son of Admiral Allen, and himself an officer in the Navy, who married, in 1792,

Catherine Manning, a clergyman's daughter; that in his will Admiral Allen termed him his son, and that the sons of this Thomas Allen, the *soi disant* "John Sobieski and Charles Edward Stuart," had respectively published a volume of poems, and had taken a wife in their proper names of Allen, thus completely ignoring their pretended royal ancestry.

Even had not direct testimony been forthcoming, the circumstantial evidence against the allegation that Prince Charles had left a legitimate child is so strong that no amount of "Romance of History" could upset it. In his latter days, when separated from his wife, the Princess Louisa, Prince Charles sent for his illegitimate daughter by Miss Walkinshaw; created her Duchess of Albany, made her mistress of his household, and left her by will almost everything that he possessed, including such family jewels and plate as were still in his possession. Not only did he omit to make any provision for, or the slightest bequest to, his supposed son and heir, but, what is still less comprehensible, neither did the Princess Louisa, the child's mother, ever appear to make any inquiry after it; nor when she died in 1824, when this pretended son must have been fifty years of age, did she give any sign that she was aware of his existence; nor did he, this son, come forward at any period of time to prove his birth and assert his parentage. After the death of Prince Charles, who, from the time of his father's decease, had borne the title of King of England, his brother, clearly ignorant of the existence of a nearer claimant to the distinction, also assumed the royal title, and caused himself to be addressed as a sovereign, and styled "Henry the Ninth, King of Great Britain and Ireland."

Many other proofs could be furnished of the utterly baseless nature of the claims of these pretenders to royalty, but it is needless; should any one desire to peruse a fuller exposition of this romance he may be referred to the number of the *Quarterly Review* already alluded to.

"John Sobieski Stuart," the elder of these claimants, died in February 1872, leaving no issue; but the younger brother, the pretended "Charles Edward Stuart," who is alleged to have received the cross of the Legion d'Honneur from the hands of the first Napoleon for bravery on the field of Waterloo, died on Christmas Eve, 1880, leaving several grown-up children, all of whom, it is believed, have assumed the pseudonym of "Stuart" and sham title of "d'Albany."

www.ingramcontent.com/pod-product-compliance
Lightning Source LLC
Chambersburg PA
CBHW031708230426
43668CB00006B/153